LEARNING

READING STRATEGIES
Comprehension Skills

Study Guide
DA 1–20

Second Edition

ISBN 1-56260-710-3

07 08 09 DBH 04 03 02

To the Student

EDL Reading Strategies lessons will help you read more easily and better understand what you read.

You will be guided through each lesson either by a cassette tape or by your teacher. You will also have the option of completing some of the activities on a computer.

Your instructor will show you how to operate the equipment. If you are working in a group, one person will be asked to serve as a group leader. The job of the group leader is to run the equipment.

If you are using a tape, listen very carefully. The narrator on the tape will introduce the new words of the lesson and explain how to use a variety of useful comprehension skills.

During each lesson, you will be asked to write the answer to exercises. Your instructor will tell you where to write the answers. The tape narrator will help you check your answers after each exercise. Correct any wrong answers you have written.

At some point during the lesson, you will be told to read a story. Your instructor will tell you whether to read the story in this book or on the computer.

At the end of each lesson, you will be told to do an exercise after the tape stops.

When you have finished this last exercise, check your answers with the key in the back of the book. Correct any wrong answers you have written. Chart your progress after each lesson.

To the Instructor

EDL Reading Strategies is available for use either with or without a cassette player or a computer. If the cassettes are used, students will receive instruction in the comprehension skills via the cassette. Otherwise, you will have to teach the skill using the directions provided in the Reading Strategies Lesson Plans DA. If the computer is used, the students will receive additional vocabulary practice along with left-to-right fluency training. The software program will also review the Word Study and Comprehension Check exercises of each Reading Strategies lesson and provide additional exercises on vocabulary.

Vocabulary Review

This edition of the Reading Strategies Study Guide contains a Vocabulary Review to reinforce the vocabulary taught in the lesson. These Vocabulary Reviews can be used either as a follow-up activity or as a posttest immediately after the lesson has been taught, or for review and reinforcement after some time has lapsed. Vocabulary Reviews begin on page 153. The Answer Key for the Vocabulary Reviews begins on page 174.

Acknowledgments

Skill Lesson Authors

Susan Bâby	Adrienne Grossberg
Melanie Belkin	Merrily P. Hansen
Arlene Block	Estelle Kleinman
George A. Corbin	Ruth Lebowitz
Ti G. Dane	Karl Weber
Judith P. Gordon	Beverly Zembko

Photographs

United Press International

Contents

Danny's Dream

_____WORD STUDY_____

a. **commanded**   Gave an order
b. **curiosity**   An eager desire to know
c. **frozen**   Unable to move

Jane's cat sits (1) _____ in the tree and hopes that my dog's

(2) _____ will soon pass. If I (3) _____ him to leave

the cat alone, he would do so.

d. **attention**   A directing of one's thoughts
e. **neighborhood** A particular area in which one's home is located
f. **weave**   To go by twisting and turning

Pay close (4) _____ when you drive in this (5) _____

because the streets (6) _____ in and out.

g. **familiar**   Well-known
h. **future**   Time that is to come
i. **purpose**   The result one aims at or arrives at
j. **realize**   To be aware of

I (7) _____ that the (8) _____ of meeting at this

(9) _____ spot is to make certain that no one gets lost. In the

(10) _____ we can meet downtown.

_____START THE PLAYER_____

Proper Noun _____

Danny _____

Danny's Dream

by Paula Potente

Danny leaned against the telephone pole near his home, an old apartment house in the part of the city known as "Hell's Kitchen." The children playing stickball in the street caught his attention. What purpose will life have for them, he wondered. What purpose will life hold for me?

Answer questions 11 and 12.

11. Where did Danny make his home?
   a. In a large kitchen
   b. In a city apartment house
   c. Beside a telephone pole
   d. In a building called "Hell's Kitchen"
12. What was Danny thinking of as he watched the children at play?
   a. Who would hit the next ball
   b. How "Hell's Kitchen" got its name
   c. How he had played stickball when he was a child
   d. What the future would be for the young people in this neighborhood

_____**START THE PLAYER**_____

COMPREHENSION CHECK

Directions: Write or circle the letter of your choice.

13. What did Danny see as his biggest problem?
    a. He no longer had a father.
    b. He had no plans for the future.
    c. His mother needed to escape.
    d. He didn't want to move east to the city.

▲14. Danny lived in a neighborhood where people
    a. bought their food from peddlers.
    b. were hopeful about their lives.
    c. had only their memories.
    d. did not have much money.

15. How did the young boys know that the lady had money in her pocketbook?
    a. They watched her leave the bank.
    b. They saw her put money away after she bought the flowers.
    c. They saw her give Danny a $50 bill.
    d. They watched her pay a bus driver.

▲16. What reason might explain why Danny was unable to move right after the boys grabbed the pocketbook?
    a. He was too surprised to realize what had happened.
    b. He was too cold to move quickly.
    c. He was too tired after his long walk.
    d. He was too busy watching the stickball game to realize what the boys had done.

17. After Danny caught the thief, he decided to
    a. let the thief go because he was so young.
    b. keep the pocketbook for himself.
    c. hide the thief from the police.
    d. hold the thief until the police arrived.

18. On his way home, Danny thought about
    a. how cold the weather was.
    b. the pretty lady whom he had helped.
    c. other young people who were in trouble.
    d. how ordinary the day had been.

19. What kind of job did Danny plan to look for?
    a. A job helping police officers
    b. A job helping older people out of work
    c. A job helping to keep young people out of trouble
    d. A job helping to teach young people exciting games like stickball

●20. This story is mainly about
    a. how a young woman's pocketbook was taken one afternoon in "Hell's Kitchen."
    b. how a young man discovered a purpose for his life.
    c. how a young man helped the police in carrying out their jobs.
    d. how city life turned a young boy into a thief.

Check your answers with the key.

START THE PLAYER

3

●●●●A●●●●

Danny leaned against the telephone pole near his home, an old apartment house in the part of the city known as "Hell's Kitchen." The children playing stickball in the street caught his attention. What purpose will life have for them, he wondered. What purpose will life hold for me?

He realized that once he finished high school, he had no plans for the future. He needed a **goal**, something to work toward. Danny started to walk.

He thought of how he'd felt when his mother told him they were moving east to the city. She said she'd had enough of his father's drinking and fighting. His mother wanted to leave. She needed to escape, and Danny understood why.

That was ten years ago. Now Danny was finishing high school. His father was only a **memory** now, someone from his past to remember now and then.

As Danny walked along, his familiar neighborhood made him sad. Everything seemed hopeless. He saw some people looking through bags that were sitting on the sidewalk. They were searching for anything **valuable** or useful. Lonely people were drinking on street corners. Danny turned off the main street and started walking east toward the river.

———————START THE PLAYER———————

21. The word **goal** as used in the story means
    a. sometime after high school.
    b. someplace to walk to.
    c. something to kick toward.
    d. something to work toward.

———————START THE PLAYER———————

22. The word **memory** as used in this story means
    a. a father who drinks and fights.
    b. a person who is remembered.
    c. a special high school.
    d. a sad thought.

———————START THE PLAYER———————

23. The word **valuable** as used in this story means
    a. something useful.
    b. something in a bag.
    c. something that lonely people do.
    d. something that is worth very little.

———————START THE PLAYER———————

••••B••••

A sudden push forward almost made him fall. When he turned, prepared for anything, he heard a quiet, "Sorry, man," and saw two young boys move by him.

They stirred Danny's curiosity, and he began to follow them. A few yards ahead, Danny noticed a pretty young woman. She bought flowers from the **peddler** who sold from his cart on the corner. The woman paid the peddler, then put her money back into her pocketbook. She continued walking.

Danny saw the two boys take off after her. He knew they were up to something from the way they were weaving through the crowd.

When the boys caught up with the woman, one pushed her and ran. The other grabbed her pocketbook and ran too. Danny stood frozen for a second, then ran madly after the boy with the pocketbook.

Danny caught up with the boy, grabbed the back of his coat, and pulled him to the ground. When Danny saw that the thief was no older than fourteen, he couldn't believe it. "Don't turn me in, man," the boy begged. "I'll give it back." Danny was **confused**. He didn't know what to do. "Please, man, no cops." The boy begged Danny to let him go, but Danny couldn't. "Give me the pocketbook," Danny commanded. As soon as Danny had the pocketbook in his hand, two police officers appeared. The young woman was right behind them.

"Thank you, son," one cop said as he shook Danny's hand. "We'll take over from here." Danny handed the young woman her pocketbook. She was so **excited**, she threw her arms around Danny and kissed him. "I want you to have this," she said. She took something out of her bag. It was a $50 bill.

Danny wouldn't **accept** the money at first. He tried to return it, but the woman stuffed the bill into his pocket. "Thank you again," she said.

24. The word *peddler* as used in this story means
    a. a person who sells flowers.
    b. a person who is pretty and young.
    c. a person who sells from a cart on the street.
    d. a person who stirred Danny's curiosity.

25. The word *confused* as used in this story means
    a. angry.
    b. certain.
    c. calm.
    d. mixed up.

26. The word *excited* as used in this story means
    a. moved to strong feelings.
    b. willing to share.
    c. lonely.
    d. curious.

_____START THE PLAYER_____

27. The word *accept* as used in this story means
    a. refuse.
    b. take.
    c. earn.
    d. spend.

_____START THE PLAYER_____

•••●C●•••

Danny turned to leave. He felt a **chill** as he looked at the boy's face, and he buttoned up his coat to keep warm. Danny started for home. Today was not an **ordinary** day in any way, he thought. It was very different. First of all, he had earned $50 for helping a pretty lady. He then began to think of that young boy and all the other young people who were in trouble too. He never had thought about that before.

It was getting dark now, and the street looked gray and empty. There were no kids playing stickball anymore.

He needed a job, and he still needed a goal. He couldn't work part-time at the gas station too much longer. . . . There must be a place in the city where kids can go for **assistance**, a place where they can get help before they get into trouble, he thought. I grew up in this city, and I know it pretty well. I'll look around tomorrow and see if I can work for a place where troubled kids can get help. He thought about it. "Keeping young kids out of trouble is a special goal to have." He said that out loud, smiled, and ran up his front steps. He suddenly realized that his mother had no idea where he'd been all day.

28. The word *chill* as used in this story means
    a. sudden fear.
    b. soft touch.
    c. warm breath.
    d. unpleasant coldness.

29. The word *ordinary* as used in this story means
    a. pleasant.
    b. usual.
    c. frightening.
    d. disappointing.

30. The word *assistance* as used in this story means
    a. clothing.
    b. money.
    c. help.
    d. food.

———START THE PLAYER———

PRACTICE

Using Context Clues

Directions: Read the story. As you read, try to figure out the meaning of each word in dark print. Then write or circle the letter that gives the correct definition.

It was a beautiful day. The sun shone brightly in the clear, blue sky, and Burt was alone in the mountains. He was on a fishing trip. He spotted a likely stream from the **peak**, or top, of a cliff. Having decided to take a closer look, he wandered too close to the edge, slipped, and fell over the side. On his way down, Burt managed to grab hold of the branch of a small tree. Far from being safe, he hung **precariously** over the seemingly endless **chasm**. A deeper, wider, and more hollow space between mountains Burt had never seen.

Burt raised his eyes to heaven and **pleaded** to the Maker-of-All-Things to save his life. No human has ever begged harder.

"O, dear Lord, help me. Help me, or I'll fall and die."

From the sky an **eerie** voice unlike that of any living being answered Burt.

"All right, my son. I'll help you. But first I must ask you a question: Do you have **faith** in me? Do you really trust me to save you?"

"O yes, Lord. I do! I do!" Burt answered.

"Very well, my son," the heavenly voice said. "Just let go of the tree branch, and you will be saved."

Burt, who was fiercely holding onto the tree branch, looked down into the bottom of the steep drop. Burt returned his eyes to the blue sky.

"Listen," he shouted, "is there anyone else up there who can help me?"

1. The word *peak* as used in this story means
   a. top.
   b. bottom.
   c. bushes.
   d. harbor.

2. The word *precariously* means
   a. by accident.
   b. in a familiar way.
   c. happily.
   d. with great danger.

3. The word *chasm* means
   a. an endless trail.
   b. a kind of rock.
   c. a bunch of mountains.
   d. a deep, wide hole.

4. The word *pleaded* means
   a. begged.
   b. stared.
   c. sang.
   d. called.

5. The word *eerie* means
   a. faraway.
   b. birdlike.
   c. very strange.
   d. deep.

6. The word *faith* means to have
   a. great fear.
   b. trust.
   c. much delight.
   d. courage.

Check your answers with the key.

_____WORD STUDY_____

a. **agree**   To share the same opinion or idea
b. **argue**   To disagree aloud
c. **business**   A matter or affair
d. **habit**   A regular practice

It is his (1) _____ to (2) _____ with people until they

feel forced to (3) _____ with his ideas. He forgets that what other

people think is none of his (4) _____.

e. **hesitate**   To hold back because of doubt or fear
f. **patiently**   Bearing trouble calmly or without complaint

If others make fun of you, it is best to bear it (5) _____, but do

not (6) _____ to stand up for yourself if you are forced to.

g. **jail**   A building where people who have broken the law are kept locked up
h. **possession**   Anything a person owns or has
i. **razor**   A sharp instrument used for shaving

The (7) _____ his father had given him was his favorite

(8) _____. It was taken away from him when he entered

(9) _____.

_____START THE PLAYER_____

Proper Nouns

Joe Palmer	Champlain	Philadelphia
East Coast	Raleigh	New York
Rocky Mountains	Pilgrims	Robert E. Lee
America	Puritans	Lincoln
Cortes	United States	Grant
Ponce de Leon	Fitchburg, Massachusetts	

_____PREVIEW_____
1. Read the title and look at the picture.
2. Read the first paragraph.
3. Then answer questions 10–12.
4. When you have finished, start the player.

The Beard of Joe Palmer

by Arthur Myers

His name was Joe Palmer, and he was a very unusual fellow. From the East Coast to the Rocky Mountains there was probably not another man like him in the early 1800s. For he may well have been the only man of his time to wear a beard.

Answer questions 10, 11, and 12.

10. What made Joe Palmer unusual?
    a. Where he lived
    b. The way he looked
    c. The time he lived
    d. His name
11. The people who saw Joe
    a. were startled by his beard.
    b. liked his beard.
    c. did not notice his beard.
    d. felt sorry for him.
12. In the early 1800s
    a. beards were common.
    b. Joe Palmer cut off his beard.
    c. Joe Palmer came to America.
    d. few Americans wore beards.

_____START THE PLAYER_____

COMPREHENSION CHECK

Directions: Write or circle the letter of your choice.

13. Joe refused to cut off his beard because he
   a. wanted to be like the Puritans.
   b. believed a man had the right to do
   as he pleased.
   c. was angry at his neighbors.
   d. liked being noticed.

14. Why did the men attack Joe?
   a. They wanted to talk him into shaving his beard.
   b. They wanted to make him leave
   town.
   c. They wanted to throw him in jail.
   d. They wanted to shave him by
   force.

15. The judge said that Joe had to go to
jail because
   a. he would not pay the fine for
   fighting.
   b. he had used a razor to attack a
   group of men.
   c. it was wrong to wear a beard.
   d. he had been carrying a knife.

▲16. When he was in jail, Joe Palmer was
   a. often visited by his family.
   b. not allowed to receive mail.
   c. carelessly guarded.
   d. not allowed to send letters freely.

▲17. The judge and the jailer wanted Joe to
leave jail when
   a. he would not cut off his beard.
   b. they saw they had been wrong.
   c. Joe's letters won many people over
   to his side.
   d. he fought with the guards in jail.

18. Joe finally left jail when
   a. the judge set him free.
   b. his mother asked him to come
   home.
   c. the jailer and his men forced him
   to go.
   d. his son got the jailer to free him.

19. Joe struck a blow for the rights of men
and women by
   a. sticking to his own way without
   giving in.
   b. fighting for a change in the laws of
   his town.
   c. attacking the people who made fun
   of him.
   d. writing stories for papers all over
   the state.

●20. This story is mainly about
   a. Joe Palmer's life behind bars.
   b. how Joe Palmer became famous.
   c. the harm that a foolish judge can
   cause.
   d. Joe Palmer's fight for the right to
   wear a beard.

Check your answers with the key.

_____ START THE PLAYER _____

10

••••A••••

His name was Joe Palmer, and he was a very unusual fellow. From the East Coast to the Rocky Mountains there was probably not another man like him in the early 1800s. For he may well have been the only man of his time to wear a beard.

Actually, the men who opened up America—Cortes, Ponce de Leon, Champlain, Raleigh—had plenty of hair on their faces. So had the Pilgrims and the Puritans. But by the early 1700s, men had completely lost the habit of such hair. The men who founded the United States were all without beards, or any other hair on their faces.

So when Joe Palmer moved into Fitchburg, Massachusetts, the town went out of its mind. Joe Palmer, then a man in his forties, wore a full beard. The beard was enough to make strong men pale, horses scream, women faint.

Children yelled mean things at Joe. Men of the cloth argued with him to get rid of his beard. Neighbors refused to speak to him.

Through it all, Joe Palmer walked patiently. He was a thinking man and a gentle man, but he never hesitated to fight off anyone who made a move toward his unusual possession. It was his business, he felt, and no one else's.

_____START THE PLAYER_____

21. _____ may have been the only man of his time to wear a

_____.

22. The habit of wearing beards had disappeared by the early _____.

23. Joe Palmer was a man in his _____ when he moved to the town of

_____.

24. Joe did not hesitate to _____ to protect his beard.

_____START THE PLAYER_____

••••B••••

As time went on, the enemies of the beard became more and more bold. One day, Joe was seized by four men armed with brush, soap, and razor. They told him that the town had made up its mind—the beard must come off. They threw him to the ground, hurting his back. But Joe had just begun to fight.

As they were about to begin work with the razor, he found a small knife in his pocket. As he struggled with the men he cut two of them in the legs. They were not hurt seriously, but they all left in a hurry. When Joe was able to get to his feet, he still had his beard.

Soon after, the police came to his home. Even though the others had started the fight, he was taken before a judge and given a small fine. He refused to pay it and was put in jail.

He remained there for more than a year. He would not pay his fine because he felt that he was in the right. The guards in the jail tried to cut off his beard, but he gave them more fight than they could handle. The beard remained.

While in jail, Joe wrote letters which he threw out the window to his son. The letters said he was being held not for fighting, but for growing a beard, which was true. Soon papers all over the state were printing his letters. People began to argue about Joe Palmer. A lot thought he was right.

The judge and the jailer now wanted Joe out of jail. But he refused to leave. His old mother wrote to him, begging him to leave the jail. He still refused. He wanted the judge to admit he had been put in jail because of his beard. The judge would not admit this. Finally, the jailer and his men put Joe in a chair. They carried him out to the street and set him down. No matter what he wanted, Joe was free.

25. Joe was seized by _____ men carrying _____,

_____, and _____, but he fought back using a small

_____.

26. Joe was kept in jail for more than _____.

27. The letters Joe wrote while in jail said he was being held for _____,

and not for _____.

28. Joe finally left jail when the _____ and _____ carried him

out in a _____.

_____START THE PLAYER_____

••••C••••

But now he was famous. People as far away as Philadelphia and New York had heard of Joe Palmer and his beard. Most people now agreed with Joe that a man's beard was no business of the state. Joe had struck a blow for the rights of man—and woman too, for that matter. After all, people argued, was America a free country or wasn't it?

He also may have struck a blow for beards. For before long, men were starting to grow them. Robert E. Lee went to war with a smooth face, but had a beard before the war ended. Lincoln became the first President to wear a beard. Grant also wore one.

Through the 1870s and 1880s, beards could be seen on face after face. Then they began to disappear. But in our own time, they have come back. Now they are all over the place. So as you look about and see the hair on so many faces, give a thought to old Joe Palmer, the man who knew what he wanted—a beard.

29. Joe's beard became famous in such far off towns as _____ and _____.

30. The first President to wear a beard was _____, and _____ grew a beard during the war.

31. Beards were common through the years of the _____ and the _____.

———START THE PLAYER———

____PRACTICE____

Reading For Facts

Directions: **Read the story. Then look back in the story to find the facts you need to fill in the blanks in the sentences below.**

Chung Lee went to his great-grandfather's door and knocked softly. He walked in and saw the old man sitting in a chair with a book in his hands. He waited for his great-grandfather to look up, and then he spoke. "What's that, sir?" Chung Lee asked, pointing to the book.

"It's a record of our family tree. This book tells the whole history of our family," Chung Lee's great-grandfather answered.

"Who was the first in our family to come to the United States?" Chung Lee asked.

His great-grandfather smiled and began: "In 1863 my grandfather, Kai-lim, was a poor farmer living in a small town in Hunan Province, China. He heard that if he would go to America, he could become rich. So, he left his family and made the very long and hard trip. In the spring of 1864, he was in San Francisco, California, working on the railroad with many of his countrymen. Years passed, and one by one he brought his family over to this country. During the hard years that followed, my grandfather and grandmother raised four sons.

"In 1890, his oldest son, my father, left California and traveled with his wife to St. Louis, Missouri. He opened a market there. My parents had three children. I was the youngest.

"By the time I was 19, in 1910, my father had saved enough money to send me to school to become a doctor. I, in turn, sent my son, your grandfather, to school to become a doctor. And his son, your father, also became a doctor. We all mixed the old Chinese ways with the new ways that we learned in school."

He smiled gently. "But I think that my father would have been happier if I had worked in the market with him," he said. Chung Lee noticed that his great-grandfather looked tired.

Chung Lee said good-bye to his great-grandfather and left the room so the old man could rest. Chung Lee smiled to himself. He wondered what his father would say when he told him that he wanted to run a supermarket instead of becoming a doctor.

1. Chung Lee asked his

_____ who was the first in the family to come to

_____ .

2. In the year _____ Kai-lim was a poor _____ living in _____ , China.

3. In the spring of _____ , Kai-lim was in _____ , working on the _____ .

4. In _____ Kai-lim's _____ son left California and moved to _____ , where he opened a

_____ .

5. Kai-lim's son had _____ children, of which Chung Lee's great-grandfather was the

_____ .

6. By the time Chung Lee's great-

grandfather was _____ , in _____ , his father had saved enough money to send him to school to become a

_____ .

7. Chung Lee's _____ and _____ also became

_____ .

Check your answers with the key.

The Girl Who Wouldn't Give Up

_____WORD STUDY_____

a. **life jacket**   Something worn to keep someone afloat in the water
b. **person**   A human being
c. **support**   Hold up

The (1) _____ who fell out of the boat was wearing a

(2) _____. It was able to (3) _____ her in the water

until help came.

d. **alligator**   A large, thick-skinned reptile that lives in the warm rivers
                       and swamps of the United States
e. **dangerous**   Not safe
f. **nature**   The manner in which a person or thing ordinarily behaves

The mean (4) _____ of an (5) _____ makes it a

(6) _____ animal.

g. **appearance**   The way someone or something looks
h. **level**   Stage of learning or achievement
i. **nurse**   A person who is trained to care for the sick

It takes a lot of training for a (7) _____ to reach the

(8) _____ where he has a happy (9) _____ even when

he feels sad.

_____START THE PLAYER_____

Proper Nouns

Kathy Miller	U.S.A.	Mrs. Miller
Scottsdale, Arizona	Olympics	

_____PREVIEW_____
1. Read the title and look at the picture.
2. Read the first paragraph.
3. Then answer questions 10 and 11.
4. When you have finished, start the player.

The Girl Who Wouldn't Give Up

by Mary Verdick

At 14, Kathy Miller of Scottsdale, Arizona, was a runner and a good one, too. Running wasn't just a hobby to Kathy. She worked hard at it, training for several hours each day. Once she came in third against 75 others her own age in a big cross-country race. She dreamed of running for the U.S.A. in the 1984 Olympics.

Answer questions 10 and 11.

10. How did Kathy train for a race?
   a. She moved to Scottsdale, Arizona.
   b. She ran several hours each day.
   c. She ran in an Olympic race.
   d. She was a good runner and didn't have to train.
11. What was Kathy's big dream?
   a. Winning a cross-country race
   b. Making running a hobby
   c. Running in the 1984 Olympics
   d. Training several hours a day

_____START THE PLAYER_____

—— COMPREHENSION CHECK ——

Directions: Write or circle the letter of your choice.

12. Where was Kathy when the accident happened?
    a. At a race
    b. At her home
    c. In a store
    d. A few blocks from home

▲13. What reason might explain why Kathy did not see the car?
    a. She was running in a race a few blocks from home.
    b. She was dreaming and did not see the car.
    c. The car was moving very quickly.
    d. The car passed a red light.

14. The doctors didn't give Kathy's parents much hope because
    a. her right leg was broken.
    b. she had been knocked right out of her shoes.
    c. her face was badly cut.
    d. she was so seriously hurt.

15. What was the first sign to show that Kathy knew what was happening around her?
    a. She nodded her head.
    b. She asked for a pillow.
    c. She smiled at a nurse.
    d. She moved to a chair.

▲16. Kathy's first sentence was important to the Miller family because it meant that she
    a. could ask for things instead of them having to guess what she needed.
    b. could call people by their names.
    c. was learning how to put words together in a way that made sense.
    d. could sing little songs again.

17. When Kathy first began to run after her accident, it took her almost an hour to run a lap because
    a. her leg was not yet completely well and it slowed her down.
    b. her running shoes no longer fit.
    c. she had to run holding her foot.
    d. she was able to run on only one leg.

18. Why did Kathy's family and friends cheer as she crossed the finish line in the November cross-country race?
    a. She had managed to finish the race even with her bad leg.
    b. She had won her first big race since the accident.
    c. She had crossed the finish line 40 minutes ahead of everyone else.
    d. She was up to the level she had been at before the accident.

●19. This story is mainly about how
    a. hard it is to walk after an accident.
    b. doctors and nurses help a sick person get well after a bad accident.
    c. a runner trains for an Olympic race.
    d. Kathy Miller worked very hard to get well after a bad accident.

Check your answers with the key.

—— START THE PLAYER ——

••••A••••

At 14, Kathy Miller of Scottsdale, Arizona, was a runner and a good one, too. Running wasn't just a hobby to Kathy. She worked hard at it, training for several hours each day. Once she came in third against 75 others her own age in a big cross-country race. She dreamed of running for the U.S.A. in the 1984 Olympics.

Then one warm March evening in 1977 Kathy almost lost her dream—along with her life. She had been shopping and was only a few blocks from her home. Suddenly a speeding car came out of the shadows.

Actually Kathy never saw the car. But it struck her so hard she was lifted right out of her shoes. She was dragged more than 50 feet.

Within seconds this strong, bright girl was lying on the side of the road in a pool of blood. Her right leg was broken in several places, her face was badly cut, and many other parts of her body were seriously hurt.

For two and a half months Kathy lay in the hospital close to death. The doctors didn't give her parents much hope. Her weight dropped from 110 pounds to 50 pounds.

Kathy couldn't see or hear or feel anything. Doctors said even if she lived she might be a "vegetable." She might never walk or talk again.

_____START THE PLAYER_____

● 20. What is the topic sentence that states the main idea of the first paragraph in Section A?
   a. At 14, Kathy Miller of Scottsdale, Arizona, was a runner and a good one, too.
   b. Running wasn't just a hobby to Kathy.
   c. She worked hard at it, training for several hours each day.
   d. She dreamed of running for the U.S.A. in the 1984 Olympics.

_____START THE PLAYER_____

● 21. What is the topic sentence that states the main idea of the rest of the paragraphs in Section A?
   a. Actually Kathy never saw the car.
   b. Kathy couldn't see or hear or feel anything.
   c. Then one warm March evening in 1977 Kathy almost lost her dream—along with her life.
   d. The doctors didn't give her parents much hope.

_____START THE PLAYER_____

B

Kathy's parents went to the hospital every day to visit their daughter. They touched her and talked to her. They played records of songs she'd liked. They refused to give up hope.

Then one day the nurses moved Kathy to a chair while they made her bed. One of the nurses put a pillow behind her back. "Feel good?" she asked. Kathy's head nodded slowly. It was the first sign Kathy gave showing she knew what was going on.

Four months later her parents took Kathy home. She was like a little baby. She had to be cleaned and fed and dressed. Mostly she just sat and stared at the wall.

● 22. What is the main idea of the first paragraph in Section B?
    a. Kathy's parents went to the hospital every day to visit their daughter.
    b. They touched her and talked to her.
    c. They played records of songs she'd liked.
    d. They refused to give up hope.

_____START THE PLAYER_____

● 23. What is the unstated main idea of the third paragraph in Section B?
    a. Kathy was very happy to be home from the hospital.
    b. At first Kathy did not get much better when she went home.
    c. Kathy liked to sit in a chair with a pillow behind her back.
    d. Kathy showed no sign of getting well until she went home.

_____START THE PLAYER_____

C

Kathy's parents kept talking to her. They sang little songs and counted to her. After a while Kathy began to make sounds herself. She learned to say Mama and Dada, dog and cat. One day she put three words together and said, "I love you." That was a great day for the Miller family.

Kathy still couldn't walk. But one day her parents put a life jacket on her and took her to a pool. At first she just lay in the water, letting the life jacket support her. Then slowly she began to move her legs. "Soon she was swimming like an alligator," Mrs. Miller said.

That was the turning point for Kathy. After that she learned how to do more and more things. Soon she could brush her teeth, comb her hair, tie her shoes. By July she was walking and even climbing stairs.

● 24. What is the unstated main idea of Section C?
    a. Kathy needed the support of a life jacket when she first started to swim.
    b. Kathy's first sentence was the turning point for her parents.
    c. Kathy's parents continued to work with her in many ways until she finally began to get well.
    d. Five months after her accident, Kathy was a better swimmer than she had been before the accident.

_____START THE PLAYER_____

●●●● **D** ●●●●

Only one big question remained: would Kathy ever run again? Kathy knew it might be dangerous but she decided to try it. She began by working out on a track near her home.

At first she would run only a few steps and then have to stop to catch her breath. It took her almost an hour to go one lap (a fourth of a mile). Her leg hurt all the time. It was still not completely well from the accident and dragged behind her when she ran. Sometimes she had to turn her leg with both hands to make it go in the right direction. That hurt so much it made her cry. But Kathy kept running.

One day Kathy was running with her father and fell. She landed on her face and broke her nose. There was blood all over her, and her eyes were black and blue. But Kathy was a brave person and even that didn't stop her. It was not in her nature to give up.

● 25. What is the main idea of Section D?
     a. Kathy found it very hard when she began to run again, but she refused to give up and continued to train.
     b. At first she would run only a few steps and then have to stop to catch her breath.
     c. Kathy often cried before, during, and after a run because her leg was not yet completely well.
     d. One day Kathy was running with her father and fell.

——— **START THE PLAYER** ———

●●●● **E** ●●●●

Kathy pushed herself more and more each day. By November, 8 months after the accident, Kathy ran in a big cross-country race again. This time she didn't cross the finish line until 40 minutes after everyone else, but to her cheering family and friends it was a wonder that she had finished at all.

Four years later, Kathy was running three hours a day and was almost up to the level she was at before the accident. She spoke slower than she used to and her right hand still shook a little, but in appearance she looked like any other pretty young woman. Because of her courage, she received hundreds of letters a week from people who wished her well, and she was even invited to the White House.

Kathy never stopped believing in herself. She used to say, "With God's help, there's nothing I can't do."

● 26. What is the main idea of Section E?
     a. Kathy was such a famous young woman that she received many letters each week from people who wished her well.
     b. She spoke slower than she used to and her right hand still shook a little, but in appearance she looked like any other pretty young woman.
     c. By November, 8 months after the accident, Kathy ran in a big cross-country race again.
     d. Kathy is a good example of how hard work, courage, and a strong will can help a person master what may seem almost impossible.

——— **START THE PLAYER** ———

PRACTICE

Reading for Main Idea

Directions: First read each part of the story. Then find the main idea of each part, and write or circle the letter of your choice.

Blanca was an expert in her field. She had worked long and hard to learn everything she could about farming. Now farmers came to her from all over the state with questions, and she almost always had the answers. If she couldn't give them an answer immediately, she did her best to find one.

● 1. What is the main idea?
   a. Blanca worked hard and long.
   b. Farmers came to Blanca with questions.
   c. Blanca was a respected expert on farming in her state.
   d. Blanca liked farming.

When she was a little girl living on her father's farm, Blanca used to help her father plant the seeds in early spring. A small piece of ground was set aside to be her garden. She cared for her plants every day and made sure that everything was done so that they would grow well.

By the time she was in high school, Blanca was winning prizes at the fairs for her plants. Three years in a row, the prize for the largest pumpkin went to her. She had blue ribbons hanging up all around her room.

● 2. What is the main idea?
   a. Blanca showed an early interest in farming, and she became very good at it by the time she was in high school.
   b. Blanca lived on her father's farm, where they planted seeds in early spring.
   c. Blanca had a garden and made sure that everything was done so the plants would grow well.
   d. Blanca won the prize for the largest pumpkin three years in a row.

At the school where Blanca studied farming, she came up with a great new food for plants. This was a food that would make the plants larger and healthier. It also would help the plants bear more fruit. The State Farming Board invited Blanca to explain this new food to them. Her father and mother were proud of their daughter.

● 3. What is the main idea?
   a. Her father and mother were proud of their daughter.
   b. At the school where Blanca studied farming, she came up with a great new food for plants.
   c. The State Farming Board invited Blanca to explain this new food to them.
   d. This was a food that would make the plants larger and healthier.

Then, on her twenty-first birthday, Blanca was in a terrible automobile accident. The doctors said that she would never walk again. Everyone wondered how Blanca would carry on with her work. It wasn't easy, but Blanca and her parents found a way.

Blanca's father bought a special pick-up truck and fixed it up so that Blanca could get in and out of the truck while in her wheelchair. They named the truck "wheels on wheels," and it soon became a familiar sight at all of the neighboring farms.

● 4. What is the main idea?
   a. The doctors said that Blanca would never walk again after her accident.
   b. Trucks can be fixed up so that you can get in and out even if you're in a wheelchair.
   c. Blanca's truck was named "wheels on wheels," and it soon became a familiar sight at all of the neighboring farms.
   d. Blanca lost the use of her legs in a terrible accident, but she managed to find a way to carry on with her work.

Check your answers with the key.

_____WORD STUDY_____

a. **champion**   Person or animal that wins first place in a game or race
b. **national**   Belonging to a nation
c. **popular**   Liked by many people

The skating (1) _____ stood on the ice while his

(2) _____ song was played. Everyone cheered for the

(3) _____ skater.

d. **distance**   The amount of space between two points
e. **language**   The speech of a country or group of people
f. **problem**   Something that causes difficulty

Fran had traveled a long (4) _____ to reach the small island.

When she arrived, she had a (5) _____ understanding the

(6) _____.

g. **control**   Have power over something
h. **mystery**   Something that is unknown
i. **upset**   Worried or disturbed

The police officer felt she was now in (7) _____ of things. She

had been (8) _____ until she'd figured out the

(9) _____ of the missing jewels.

_____START THE PLAYER_____

Proper Nouns

Miruts Yifter	Olympic Games	New Zealand
Ethiopia	South Africa	African

_____PREVIEW_____
1. Read the title and look at the picture.
2. Read the first paragraph.
3. Then answer questions 10 and 11.
4. When you have finished, start the player.

The Mystery Man

by Daniel J. Domoff

People called him the "mystery man" of track and field. But Miruts Yifter really was no mystery. Anyone who was a fan of track and field knew that Miruts Yifter was one of the finest distance runners in the world. And people also knew just what Yifter would do in any race he ran. He would stay right up with the leaders all the way. He never seemed to tire. But then, as the leaders entered the last lap of the race, Miruts Yifter would turn on the speed and run away from them all. This last-lap "kick" would, time after time, beat the world's best runners. Yifter always ran this way, and he always won.

10. Who is Miruts Yifter?
   a. A swimmer
   b. A fan
   c. A runner
   d. A world leader
11. What was he known for?
   a. Writing mystery stories about track and field
   b. Kicking people when he raced
   c. Keeping the field in fine shape
   d. Turning on the speed in the last lap of a race

Answer questions 10 and 11.

_____START THE PLAYER_____

23

●●●●A●●●●

People called him the "mystery man" of track and field. But Miruts Yifter really was no mystery. Anyone who was a fan of track and field knew that Miruts Yifter was one of the finest distance runners in the world. And people also knew just what Yifter would do in any race he ran. He would stay right up with the leaders all the way. He never seemed to tire. But then, as the leaders entered the last lap of the race, Miruts Yifter would turn on the speed and run away from them all. This last-lap "kick" would, time after time, beat the world's best runners. Yifter always ran this way, and he always won.

So why was he called a "mystery man"? Because most press and television people couldn't speak with him. Miruts Yifter spoke only the language of his country, Ethiopia. In Ethiopia, he was a national hero and a popular man. But in other countries, Miruts Yifter was known only as a short, thin runner with a great kick.

All good runners know that they must not start their kicks too soon. If they do, they could lose their speed before the end of the race, and the other runners would beat them. In 1971 Miruts Yifter was in a 5,000-meter race (3.1 miles). It was near the end of the race. As always, Yifter was running with the leaders. He felt that he was in control of the race. As the runners finished a lap, one of the track judges called out, "Two laps to go!" But Miruts Yifter didn't understand the language. He thought that the judge was saying that there was only one lap to go. So Miruts Yifter began his kick.

———— START THE PLAYER ————

12. What do all good runners know?
    a. They should slow down before the end of a race.
    b. They shouldn't start their kicks too soon.
    c. They should run as fast as they can from the beginning of a race.
    d. They should start their kicks as soon as possible.

13. In the 5,000-meter race, what did Miruts do?
    a. He got mad at another runner.
    b. He ran ahead of the leaders.
    c. He began his kick with two laps to go.
    d. He lost control of himself.

14. Why did he do this?
    a. He did not understand the judge.
    b. He was tired.
    c. Someone hit him.
    d. He was told to run ten laps.

———— START THE PLAYER ————

▲ 15. How would you predict the outcome of the race?
    a. Miruts will fall down.
    b. Miruts will win.
    c. Miruts will lose.
    d. Miruts will tie for first place.

———— START THE PLAYER ————

••••B•••••

He had kicked too soon. By the time Yifter realized his mistake, he had run a full lap at top speed. Then he stopped, thinking the race was over. But there was still one more lap to go! All the other runners passed him.

Miruts Yifter was upset. But he was even more upset at the 1972 Olympic Games. He got lost on his way to the start of the 5,000–meter run. He missed the race. Now he would have to wait four more years for another chance to be an Olympic champion.

But four years later, in 1976, a problem came up. It had nothing to do with running. Instead, it was a problem among nations.

In the past, the nation of South Africa was not allowed to go to the Olympics. This was because black South Africans were kept apart from white South Africans. And so the nations of the world did not allow South Africa to take part in the Olympic Games.

Before the 1976 Olympics, a team from New Zealand had played a game in South Africa. This made many other nations angry. Most of these nations were African. "New Zealand should not be allowed in the Olympics," they said. "If New Zealand goes to the Olympics, we will not take part in the Games."

But New Zealand was allowed to go to the Olympics. And in the African nation of Ethiopia, a runner named Miruts Yifter wondered what would happen.

_____ **START THE PLAYER** _____

16. What did many African nations say they would do if New Zealand went to the 1976 Olympics?
    a. They would ask that South Africa go too.
    b. They would support New Zealand.
    c. They would not take part in the games.
    d. They would also go to the games.

17. What happened to New Zealand's team?
    a. They were not allowed to go to the Olympics.
    b. They were allowed to go.
    c. They walked out on the games.
    d. They won at the Olympics.

_____ **START THE PLAYER** _____

▲18. What will happen to Miruts Yifter in 1976?
    a. He'll get lost at the Olympics.
    b. He'll win at the Olympics.
    c. He'll lose at the Olympics.
    d. He won't go to the Olympics.

_____ **START THE PLAYER** _____

25

••••C••••

The angry nations kept their promise. They did not take part in the Olympic Games. Ethiopia's team stayed home. And Miruts Yifter's hopes of winning at the Olympics would now have to wait until 1980.

But by 1980, Miruts Yifter would be 36. For a runner, even a great one, that is "old." Would Yifter still be able to run as he had when he was younger? Would he still have his great kick? Would he be good enough to go to the Olympics at all?

So for four more years, Miruts Yifter trained hard. The great distance runner ran and ran. He trained to keep up his speed for his kick. He also learned how to understand the judges' lap calls. No more mistakes! And by the time the 1980 Olympics arrived, Miruts Yifter, who had waited so long, was ready.

_____START THE PLAYER_____

19. What problem would face Miruts Yifter in 1980?
    a. Ethiopia would not take part in the Olympics.
    b. He would be "old" for a runner.
    c. He would not understand the judge's calls.
    d. He would not be ready to run.

20. What did Miruts do to get ready for the 1980 Olympics?
    a. He trained hard.
    b. He gained weight.
    c. He slept a lot.
    d. He learned to understand the judges' lap calls.

▲ 21. What do you think will happen to Miruts Yifter in the 1980 Olympics?
    a. He won't go to the Olympics.
    b. He will win the race.
    c. He will get lost again.
    d. He will lose the race.

_____START THE PLAYER_____

••••D••••

Yifter was entered in both the 5,000-meter run and the 10,000-meter run (6.2 miles). Even at the age of 36, he knew he had a good chance to win one, if not both. But the other runners were not stupid. They knew about Yifter's kick. They, too, had practiced their kicks. And in each race, the other runners kept their eyes on Yifter.

The other runners had their plans. Some tried to make Yifter run fast early in the race, so that he wouldn't be so strong at the end. Others waited for the last lap. They would try to outkick Miruts Yifter.

But nothing they did mattered. In both races, Miruts Yifter outkicked them all. The "mystery man" was, at last, an Olympic champion.

_____START THE PLAYER_____

COMPREHENSION CHECK

Directions: Write or circle the letter of your choice.

22. Why was Miruts Yifter called the mystery man?
    a. Because he wrote mystery stories
    b. Because he ran away from everyone
    c. Because he could only speak the language of his country
    d. Because he was never seen

23. Where was Miruts Yifter from?
    a. South Africa
    b. Ethiopia
    c. New Zealand
    d. America

24. Why wasn't South Africa allowed to go to the Olympics?
    a. Because it had no sports teams
    b. Because blacks and whites were kept apart in that country
    c. Because it didn't have enough money
    d. Because it won in the last Olympics

25. Why were the African nations angry at New Zealand?
    a. New Zealand played a game in South Africa.
    b. New Zealand had a winning team.
    c. New Zealand was bigger than Africa.
    d. Africa and New Zealand were at war.

26. What happened to Miruts Yifter at the 1972 Olympics?
    a. He began his kick too soon.
    b. He won the 5,000–meter race.
    c. He got lost and missed the race.
    d. He had a fight.

▲ 27. How do you think he felt during the 1976 Olympics?
    a. Happy
    b. Upset
    c. Lonely
    d. Carefree

28. How old was Miruts at the 1980 Olympics?
    a. 25
    b. 50
    c. 31
    d. 36

29. When the 1980 Olympics arrived, Miruts Yifter
    a. was too old to enter the Olympics.
    b. no longer had his great kick.
    c. was ready to run.
    d. could not run as he had when he was younger.

30. In the 1980 races, the runners
    a. kept their eyes on Yifter.
    b. were happy that Yifter was not running.
    c. let Yifter win.
    d. ran faster than Yifter.

● 31. This story is mainly about
    a. the Olympics.
    b. New Zealand and South Africa.
    c. language problems people have.
    d. a runner trying to become a champion.

Check your answers with the key.

Go on to the next page.

PRACTICE

Predicting Outcomes

Directions: Read each part of the story. Then answer the questions by writing or circling the letter of your choice.

Long ago in a faraway land lived four men who were lifelong friends. Three of them had learned all there was to learn. The fourth, Rollo, had never gone to school; Rollo had only everyday wisdom.

One day all four of them met, and the three learned ones asked each other: "What's the good of all our learning if we don't get the good will of the king? He's the only one who can make us rich and famous."

1. The learned men want to
    a. become rulers of the country.
    b. lead a simple, quiet life.
    c. build a great school.
    d. become rich and famous.

▲ 2. What will the four friends do next?
    a. Read more books
    b. Sit around and argue
    c. Travel to see the king
    d. Write a great book

They decided to go see the king. After they had traveled a stretch, they came upon the bones of a lion.

The oldest learned man said: "Here's a chance to practice our great learning. Let's bring this lion back to life."

"Good idea," said the other two learned friends.

"I can put the bones together," said the first.

"I know how to give it skin and blood," said the second.

"And I know how to give it life," said the third.

"Hold it, guys," said Rollo. "Live lions are dangerous. They kill people—that's us."

"You're very simpleminded, Rollo," said the first. "What good is all our learning if we never use it?"

3. The three learned men want to
    a. catch a live lion for the king.
    b. forget all they ever learned.
    c. die young—together.
    d. practice what they've learned.

▲ 4. What will happen next?
    a. They'll bring the lion back to life.
    b. They'll let the dead lion stay dead.
    c. They'll teach Rollo how to train a lion.
    d. They'll ask Rollo to go home because he's a coward.

"Does that mean you're going to bring the lion back to life?" Rollo asked.

"Yes!" the others answered.

"OK," said Rollo. "Just give me time to climb that tree first."

When Rollo was in the tree, the others brought the lion back to life.

▲ 5. What will happen next?
    a. The lion will not harm the three men who saved him.
    b. Rollo will fall out of the tree into the lion's mouth.
    c. The lion will eat the three learned men.
    d. Rollo will train the lion to do tricks for the king.

Finish the story to see if your prediction comes true.

The lion rose up and, being hungry, killed the three learned men for his dinner. After the lion left, Rollo climbed down the tree and went home.

Check your answers with the key.

Hostage! **Reading for Main Idea and Supporting Details**

____WORD STUDY____

a. **program** — A plan of what is to be done
b. **develop** — To work out in detail
c. **condition** — A state of health
d. **strength** — The quality of being strong

Some of the football players were not in very good (1) _____. The

coach told them to (2) _____ an exercise (3) _____.

This, he said, would help build up their (4) _____.

e. **rise** — To get out of bed
f. **immediately** — At once

When I (5) _____ each morning, I am so hungry that I

(6) _____ go into the kitchen for breakfast.

g. **avoid** — To keep away from
h. **defend** — To protect
i. **tear gas** — A gas that irritates the eyes, causing temporary blindness
j. **hostage** — A person who is held by an enemy until certain requirements are met

The (7) _____ tried to (8) _____ the

(9) _____ thrown into the building by the police, but he had no

way to (10) _____ himself.

_____START THE PLAYER_____

Proper Nouns

Teheran, Iran	Iranians	French
Richard Queen	Mushroom Inn	United States
American Embassy	Mars	

_____ **PREVIEW** _____
1. Read the title and look at the picture.
2. Read the first paragraph.
3. Then answer questions 11 and 12.
4. When you have finished, start the player.

Hostage!

by Mary Verdick

It was Sunday morning, November 4, 1979. The place was Teheran, Iran. A young American, Richard Queen, along with ten other Americans, was working at his desk in the American Embassy. Suddenly he heard shouting and loud noises outside.

Answer questions 11 and 12.

11. What were the Americans doing at the American Embassy in Iran?
    a. They were visiting.
    b. They were working.
    c. They were making loud noises and shouting.
    d. They were holding a party.

▲12. This story will probably be about
    a. what it's like to work in an embassy.
    b. what it's like to live in Iran.
    c. a young Iranian who worked in the American Embassy.
    d. One of the hostages taken in Iran.

_____ **START THE PLAYER** _____

——COMPREHENSION CHECK——

Directions: Write or circle the letter of your choice.

13. How did the Iranians get near the American Embassy building?
    a. They shouted until the Americans let them in.
    b. They crept in through the back door.
    c. They threw tear gas into the open windows.
    d. They crashed through the gate and climbed over the walls.

14. How did the Americans try to keep the Iranians out of the embassy?
    a. By blasting the Iranians on the roof with tear gas
    b. By sitting in darkness
    c. By boarding up all the doors and windows
    d. By letting them go to other buildings at the embassy

▲15. How do you think the Iranians felt about the Americans?
    a. They felt grateful that the Americans were working in Iran.
    b. They liked Americans.
    c. They didn't care that the Americans were working at the embassy.
    d. They did not like Americans.

▲16. Why do you think that life inside the Mushroom Inn was like living on Mars?
    a. The Americans were cut off from life outside while they stayed there.
    b. It was very dark there.
    c. The Iranian language sounded as strange as a language from Mars.
    d. There was too much to see and hear there.

17. Things got better for the Americans when they were moved to a large office building because
    a. there was a window there and they were allowed to talk to each other.
    b. they went outside every day.
    c. they were able to study French there.
    d. they were able to get back to work.

18. Why couldn't Queen enjoy his new home in the office building?
    a. He had to share his room there.
    b. He couldn't study French.
    c. He wasn't allowed to go outside.
    d. He wasn't feeling well.

19. Why did Queen become ill with multiple sclerosis?
    a. He spent too much time inside the Mushroom Inn.
    b. Nobody knows why he became ill.
    c. He never went outside.
    d. His hands were tied for many months.

●20. This story is mainly about
    a. Richard Queen's hostage experiences in Iran.
    b. why the Iranians took the American hostages.
    c. what life was like inside the Mushroom Inn.
    d. the reason Richard Queen became very ill.

Check your answers with the key.

——**START THE PLAYER**——

●●●●●**A**●●●●

It was Sunday morning, November 4, 1979. The place was Teheran, Iran. A young American, Richard Queen, along with ten other Americans, was working at his desk in the American Embassy. Suddenly he heard shouting and loud noises outside.

Queen ran to the window. He saw a crowd of angry Iranians crashing through the embassy gate and climbing over the walls. Next he heard feet running across the roof. Then an Iranian kicked in a window. One of the Marine guards blasted him with a shot of tear gas. The Iranian's eyes watered and he quickly backed off.

Queen and the other Americans lost no time boarding up all the doors and windows. That's about all they could do. They had no way to defend themselves. Then the lights went out. They sat in darkness for three hours listening to the angry crowd outside. The crowd was busy taking over the other buildings at the embassy. Finally Queen and his friends decided to make a break for it. What did they have to lose?

They crept out the back door and made it to the street. There the eleven Americans decided to split up. Five went down one street and got away. Queen's group of six chose another route and were caught before they had gone three blocks. Queen was one of 53 Americans taken hostage in Teheran that day.

● 21. What is the main idea?
    a. The Americans were working at the American Embassy in Iran.
    b. The Marine guard blasted an Iranian with tear gas.
    c. The Americans were taken hostage in Iran.
    d. The Americans crept out the back door of the embassy.

—————START THE PLAYER———

22. For each question, write the letter of the supporting detail that answers it.
    1._____ **When** were the hostages taken?
    2._____ **Where** were they when taken?
    3._____ **Who** took them hostage?
    4._____ **How** did Queen first see the crowd?
    5._____ **How** did the Iranians get near the embassy?
    6._____ **How** did the Americans keep them out?
    7._____ **How** did the Americans try to get away?
    8._____ **How** many hostages in all were taken?

    a. Fifty-three
    b. He looked out the window.
    c. They crept out the back door.
    d. They crashed the gate and climbed the walls.
    e. A crowd of Iranians
    f. By boarding up the windows and doors
    g. November 4, 1979
    h. At the American Embassy in Iran

—————START THE PLAYER———

•••• B ••••

Queen's hands were tied behind his back. Strips of cloth covered his eyes. He was dragged back to the embassy.

The next day his guards took the blinds from Queen's eyes, but he remained tied to the chair he sat in for five days. Even after the guards untied him from the chair, his hands were kept tied for many months.

As if that wasn't bad enough, Queen was placed in an underground building. "Immediately, we named it the Mushroom Inn," Queen said. "It had no windows; it was like a cellar. There was nothing to see but the walls."

There was nothing to hear in the Mushroom, either. Because it was underground, no sounds got through. It was like living on Mars. The lights were kept on, but there was no real way of telling if it was day or night.

Queen was locked in a room with another American hostage, but they were not allowed to talk to each other. A guard with a machine gun sat outside in the hall and watched them every moment.

Queen understood some Iranian words and could hear the guards talking among themselves. What he heard frightened him.

His mind started playing strange tricks on him. "Many times I thought we were going to be shot," he said. "I didn't see how we could avoid it."

To keep from going nuts, Queen developed a program of study. Luckily there were books in the Mushroom. Queen would rise early in the morning and study French. He studied French for hours at a time and taught himself to read it very well.

After many weeks underground, Queen and the others were taken outside one day for fifteen minutes. "They made us put blankets over our heads," Queen said. "When we got to a certain place between the buildings, they told us to take the blankets off and look around. There wasn't much to see—just a few trees and the sky. But nature was so beautiful, I cried. We all cried a little that day."

In March things got a little better. Queen was moved from the Mushroom Inn to a large office building. He and the American sharing the room with him were allowed to talk to each other now. Best of all, they had a room with a window.

● 23. What is the main idea?
   a. Queen was tied to a chair for five days.
   b. Queen and the other hostages went through hard times.
   c. Richard Queen taught himself to speak French.
   d. Richard Queen thought the Iranians were going to shoot him.

_____START THE PLAYER_____

24. For each question, write the letter of the supporting detail that answers it.
   1._____ **How** long were Queen's hands tied?
   2._____ **What** was the name given to the place where the hostages stayed?
   3._____ **Where** was this place?
   4._____ **Who** was in the room with Queen?
   5._____ **Who** was outside in the hall?
   6._____ **What** was Queen afraid the Iranians were going to do?
   7._____ **What** did Queen study?
   8._____ **When** were the Americans taken outside?
   9._____ **What** did the Americans see outside?

   a. After many weeks underground
   b. Shoot him and the others
   c. Trees and the sky
   d. For many months
   e. The Mushroom Inn
   f. Another hostage
   g. In an underground building
   h. French
   i. An Iranian guard

_____START THE PLAYER_____

●●●●C●●●●

But Queen couldn't enjoy his new "home." He just wasn't feeling well. He began to see two of everything, and he had trouble keeping food down. But worst of all, he had lost all his strength. He couldn't even stand without falling. He had lost all feeling in the left side of his body. When he tried to pick up something with his left hand, it would fall right out of his fingers.

Queen knew his condition was serious and he asked his guards for help. One day a guard came with an Iranian doctor. The doctor took one look at Queen and said, "Get this man to the hospital!"

At the hospital the doctors gave Queen a battery of tests, but they couldn't find out what was wrong. So after four days in the hospital, the Iranian government let Queen go home to the United States.

The doctors in the United States found that Queen had an illness called multiple sclerosis. If Queen had never been held hostage, would he have become ill? Nobody knows for sure.

Shortly after Queen was let go, he said, "I'll never be really happy until the other 52 Americans are free, too."

On January 20, 1981, 444 days after they were first taken, all of the hostages were finally set free. Queen's happiness was now complete.

● 25. What is the main idea?
   a. Queen lost all of his strength.
   b. The Iranian doctor put Queen in the hospital.
   c. The doctors in Iran did not know what Queen's illness was.
   d. Queen became ill and was allowed to return home.

―――――START THE PLAYER―――――

26. For each question, write the letter of the supporting detail that answers it.

   1.＿＿＿＿ **Why** couldn't Queen enjoy his new "home"?
   2.＿＿＿＿ **What** was the worst part of Queen's illness?
   3.＿＿＿＿ **Who** did Queen ask for help?
   4.＿＿＿＿ **Where** was Queen taken first?
   5.＿＿＿＿ **How** long was he there?
   6.＿＿＿＿ **Where** did the Iranian government send Queen?
   7.＿＿＿＿ **What** disease did Queen have?
   8.＿＿＿＿ **Who** found out what was wrong with Queen?
   9.＿＿＿＿ **How** long was Queen held hostage?

   a. Multiple sclerosis
   b. The guards
   c. The American doctors
   d. He lost all his strength.
   e. Five months
   f. To an Iranian hospital
   g. Home to the United States
   h. Four days
   i. He wasn't feeling well.

―――――START THE PLAYER―――――

_____PRACTICE_____

Reading for Main Idea and Supporting Details

Directions: Read the story. Then answer the questions.

At 12:18 P.M. on February 26, 1993, a blast rocked the World Trade Center in New York City. Six people died and over 1,000 were hurt. The blast caused a hole 100 feet across and three stories deep, the work of people from another country who wanted to spread fear in the United States. But what stands out is not the fear but the courage of the common person.

As fire fighter Kevin Shea inched his way across the parking garage where the blast took place, the floor gave way. He fell four floors into the hole, breaking his left leg and right foot. Shea couldn't move to avoid the rocks falling from above.

Coming down from the 107th floor, teacher Anne Marie Tesoriero was stuck in a dark, smokey elevator with 17 young children. "We told them not to worry, but the little ones really missed the light," she said. Tesoriero thought of the children first, having them sing songs and play games to keep them calm.

On the 37th floor, Joseph Gibney was sitting in his wheelchair eating lunch when the blast went off. Two fellow workers named Jack and Andy started to carry Gibney down the stairs. When Andy's strength gave out, a young Asian man took over for him, shouting over and over, "We're going to make it."

What happened to these people? Fire fighter Joe Ward found Shea, and other fire fighters helped raise him out of the hole. After five hours, teacher Tesoriero and her young charges were saved when fire fighters chopped a hole in the side of the elevator. And Gibney also made it down to safety, thanks to caring people who kept their heads in the face of danger.

● 1. What is the main idea?
   a. People from other countries want to spread fear in the United States.
   b. As fire fighter Kevin Shea inched his way across the parking garage where the blast took place, the floor gave way.
   c. The way people acted after the World Trade Center blast showed the courage of the common person.
   d. Six people died and over 1,000 were hurt in the World Trade Center blast.

2. For each question, write the letter of the supporting detail that answers it.

1. _____ **When** did the blast take place?
2. _____ **Where** was Kevin Shea when he fell into the hole?
3. _____ **Who** was stuck in an elevator with 17 children?
4. _____ **What** did she do to keep the children calm?
5. _____ **What** was Joseph Gibney sitting in?
6. _____ **How** did he get down the stairs?
7. _____ **Who** found Kevin Shea?

a. He was carried.
b. Joe Ward
c. She had them sing songs and play games.
d. Anne Marie Tesoriero
e. At 12:18 P.M. on February 26, 1993
f. A wheelchair
g. In the parking garage

Check your answers with the key.

——WORD STUDY——

a. **silence**   To keep under restraint or control
b. **union**   A group of workers joined together to protect their interests
c. **boss**   A person who hires workers or watches over them

My (1) _____ doesn't like the fact that his workers have

united, and he has tried his best to (2) _____ their

(3) _____ .

d. **creature**   Any living person or animal
e. **dozen**   A group of twelve
f. **peaceful**   Quiet or calm

My wife loves her cat, but I can't stand the (4) _____. Things were

a lot more (5) _____ before it came to live with us. They say a cat

has nine lives—since I'm not lucky, this one will probably have more than a

(6) _____ .

g. **cheerful**   Full of good spirits
h. **vanish**   Disappear suddenly
i. **ghost**   A spirit of one who is dead

My uncle was a (7) _____ man, always seeing the bright side

of things. Maybe that's why I was not upset when his (8) _____

came to me late one night. After a nice visit, my uncle just seemed to

(9) _____ into thin air.

——START THE PLAYER——

Proper Nouns

Chico Mendes	Euclides Távora	Xapuri
Amazon	Brazil	United States

_____ PREVIEW _____
1. Read the title and look at the picture.
2. Read the first paragraph.
3. Then answer questions 10 and 11.
4. When you have finished, start the player.

The Fight to Save the Forest

by Estelle Kleinman

Chico Mendes was a short, stout man with a cheerful nature. He loved the Amazon rain forest, where he lived and worked as a rubber tapper. A rubber tapper collects the milky juice, known as latex, that flows from the bark of the rubber tree when it's cut. Respecting the forest and the creatures that live there, rubber tappers are careful not to harm the trees. But there are others who don't care about the forest. It was with these people that Chico Mendes would be in the fight of his life.

Answer questions 10 and 11.

10. Write the letters of **all** the things that are true about rubber tappers.
    a. They collect latex from the bark of rubber trees.
    b. They don't care about the forest.
    c. They work in the rain forest.
    d. They are careful not to harm the trees.
    e. They live and work in big cities.

▲ 11. The fight of Chico Mendes's life will probably be
    a. to save the rain forest.
    b. to get enough money to leave the rain forest.
    c. to be something more than a rubber tapper.
    d. to clear the rain forest to make way for farms.

_____ **START THE PLAYER** _____

_____ COMPREHENSION CHECK _____

Directions: Write or circle the letter of your choice.

12. In what ways did bosses control the rubber tappers? (Write or circle the letters of **all** correct answers.)
    a. Bosses didn't let the rubber tappers marry.
    b. Bosses forced the rubber tappers to buy goods and get homes from them.
    c. Rubber tappers had to sell all their rubber to the bosses.
    d. Bossses didn't let children of rubber tappers go to school.
    e. Rubber tappers worked for no pay at all.

13. Who gave Mendes the idea of uniting the rubber tappers in a strong union?
    a. His father
    b. His wife
    c. Euclides Távora
    d. A union president

14. What events led Mendes to believe that the forest was in danger? (Write or circle the letters of **all** correct answers.)
    a. Trees were plowed down to make way for a highway.
    b. Rubber tappers no longer took care when collecting latex.
    c. City families burned large stretches of forest for farmland.
    d. A cold winter caused people to cut down trees for firewood.
    e. Cattle ranchers burned or cut down over 1,000,000 trees.
    f. Trees were dying because there wasn't enough rain.

▲ 15. Why did the danger to the forest serve to unite the rubber tappers?
    a. They knew that without rubber trees, they would have no work.
    b. They didn't like the city families who were coming in.
    c. They hunted the animals that lived in the forest for food.
    d. They needed the trees for firewood to keep them warm.

16. How did Mendes save large parts of the forest?
    a. He used guns to make workers stop cutting down trees.
    b. He set fire to the houses of workers who cut down trees.
    c. He damaged the chain saws used to cut down trees.
    d. He formed "people fences" around workers cutting down trees until they put down their saws and left.

▲ 17. Why did the cattle ranchers try to silence the union supporters?
    a. They knew that the union didn't have the best interests of the forest at heart.
    b. They were afraid they would lose money if they were stopped from clearing the forest for their cattle.
    c. They knew that the union supporters wanted to take over the cattle ranches.
    d. They were afraid that the union would try to kill them.

18. Mendes was killed the same year that
    a. the union set up schools for the first time.
    b. the Brazilian government agreed to set aside part of the rain forest where trees could be safe.
    c. a national meeting of rubber tappers was held.
    d. two cattle ranchers got 19 years behind bars for his death.

● 19. This story is mainly about
    a. the work of a rubber tapper.
    b. the government of Brazil.
    c. one man's fight to save the rain forest.
    d. the power of a union.

Check your answers with the key.

_____ **START THE PLAYER** _____

••••● A ●•••

Chico Mendes was a short, stout man with a cheerful nature. He loved the Amazon rain forest, where he lived and worked as a rubber tapper. A rubber tapper collects the milky juice, known as latex, that flows from the bark of the rubber tree when it's cut. Respecting the forest and the creatures that live there, rubber tappers are careful not to harm the trees. But there are others who don't care about the forest. It was with these people that Chico Mendes would be in the fight of his life.

The living conditions for rubber tappers had always been poor. Being forced to buy goods and get their homes from their bosses, the tappers never saw much of their hard-earned money. They also had to sell their rubber to the bosses, who often didn't pay them enough. The bosses didn't allow the children of tappers to go to school, fearing they would soon discover they were being tricked.

Chico was a bright boy, first learning a little reading and counting from his father and then learning more on his own. Soon he met a man named Euclides Távora, who taught young Mendes about the struggles of workers all over the world. It was from Távora that Mendes got the idea of uniting the rubber tappers in a strong union. In 1968 he tried to do just that, but people weren't interested. Little did he know that coming events would serve to unite his people more than he ever could.

In 1969 the government of Brazil made plans to help poor city families move to the forest by offering them land, a house, and weekly pay to farm the land. The government also asked ranchers to clear the forest and raise cattle. Between 1969 and 1975 the rain forest was under attack from all sides. First, trees were plowed down to make way for a highway. Next, the city families who traveled that highway burned large stretches of forest for farmland, using up the land before moving on. But even worse were the cattle ranchers, who burned or cut down over 1,000,000 trees.

_____ START THE PLAYER _____

20. Number the events to show the correct sequence.
   a. _____ The government of Brazil planned to help poor city families move to the forest, and have ranchers raise cattle there.
   b. _____ Chico met a man named Euclides Távora.
   c. _____ Trees were plowed down to make way for a highway.
   d. _____ Mendes tried to unite the rubber tappers in a strong union.
   e. _____ Chico learned a little reading and counting from his father, and then learned more on his own.
   f. _____ City families burned large stretches of the forest for farmland, and cattle ranchers burned or cut down over 1,000,000 trees.

_____ START THE PLAYER _____

••• B•••

Chico Mendes feared that the rain forest would soon vanish and rubber tappers would be out of work. He made up his mind to fight to save the forest. Mendes joined a national workers' union in 1975. Then he ran for office in his town of Xapuri and won. Now a leader of his people, Mendes found he had little time to tap rubber.

In 1976 Mendes led a group of rubber tappers into the forest to where workers were cutting down trees. The tappers were peaceful, but they formed a circle around the workers and would not break it. Three days later the workers put down their chain saws and left. This was the first of dozens of such "people fences" that helped save large parts of the forest.

Mendes and the rubber tappers formed a union right in Xapuri in 1977. As this group grew in strength, the ranchers decided to silence them. Union supporters found their houses set on fire, and they feared for their lives. But they didn't stop their fight.

_____ START THE PLAYER _____

21. Number the events to show the correct sequence.
    a. _____ Mendes feared that soon the rain forest would vanish and the rubber tappers would be out of work.
    b. _____ Mendes found he had little time to tap rubber.
    c. _____ Mendes made up his mind to fight to save the forest.
    d. _____ Mendes ran for office in Xapuri and won.
    e. _____ Mendes joined a national workers' union.

_____ START THE PLAYER _____

22. Number the events to show the correct sequence.
    a. _____ The workers put down their chain saws and left.
    b. _____ Mendes and the rubber tappers formed a union right in Xapuri.
    c. _____ The tappers formed a circle around the workers and would not break it.
    d. _____ The ranchers decided to silence the union.
    e. _____ Mendes led a group of rubber tappers into the forest to where workers were cutting down trees.

_____ START THE PLAYER _____

•••● C ●•••

In 1979 the union set up the first schools for rubber tappers' children. At the same time, more and more people joined Mendes's "people fences." To strike back, the ranchers killed the union president in 1980. Instead of stopping the union, this hateful act only served to make it stronger.

At a national meeting of tappers in 1985, Mendes developed a plan for setting aside parts of the rain forest where trees would be safe. In these parts, goods such as latex and nuts could be taken without harming the trees. After this meeting, countries around the world joined the fight to save the rain forest. In 1987 Mendes went to the United States to get needed support for his struggle.

In 1988 the Brazilian government agreed to set aside part of the rain forest as Mendes had wished. This was a great victory, but it also meant greater danger. More union supporters were being killed every day. Having a wife and two young children, Mendes didn't want to die. Yet he declared, "We can't run away from this fight."

In the winter of 1988, Mendes was killed just outside his house. Word of his death spread around the world, and more than a thousand people showed up to pay their last respects. In 1990 two cattle ranchers got 19 years behind bars for killing Mendes.

Today people all over the world are working to save the rain forest. A friend of Mendes's said of him, "Chico is alive in the things that he did, the things he stood for." Some believe the ghost of Chico Mendes still looks out for the rain forest he loved.

———— START THE PLAYER ————

23. Number the events to show the correct sequence.
    a. _____ Countries around the world joined the fight to save the rain forest.
    b. _____ The union set up schools for the first time.
    c. _____ Mendes developed a plan for setting aside parts of the rain forest where trees would be safe.
    d. _____ The ranchers killed the union president.
    e. _____ Mendes went to the United States to get needed support for his struggle.

———— START THE PLAYER ————

24. Number the events to show the correct sequence.
    a. _____ Mendes declared, "We can't run away from this fight."
    b. _____ Word of Mendes's death spread around the world, and more than a thousand people showed up to pay their last respects.
    c. _____ Mendes was killed just outside his house.
    d. _____ Two cattle ranchers got 19 years behind bars for killing Mendes.
    e. _____ The government of Brazil set aside a part of the rain forest as Mendes had wished.

———— START THE PLAYER ————

_____PRACTICE_____

Reading for Sequence of Events

Directions: Read the story section by section. Then do the exercises.

Sacagawea, the daughter of a Shoshone chief, was born in Idaho in 1787. When she was 13, an enemy tribe, the Hidatsa, stole her from her people. Soon afterward they sold her to a French Canadian named Toussaint Charbonneau. Charbonneau bought Sacagawea because he wanted someone to work for him and take care of his home without having to pay the worker. In 1804, when Meriwether Lewis and William Clark decided to make a trail from the Rocky Mountains to the Pacific Ocean, they hired Charbonneau as a guide. He said that he would not go without Sacagawea. Lewis and Clark agreed to let Sacagawea come because they knew that she could help them talk to the Native Americans they would meet along the way.

1. Number the events to show the correct sequence.
   a. _____ Lewis and Clark hired Charbonneau as a guide.
   b. _____ The Hidatsa stole Sacagawea from her people.
   c. _____ Sacagawea was born in Idaho.
   d. _____ Lewis and Clark agreed to let Sacagawea go on the trip.
   e. _____ The Hidatsa sold Sacagawea to Charbonneau.

The trip across the Rocky Mountains began on April 17, 1805. Sacagawea brought along her baby son. He was only two months old at the time. William Clark became very fond of Sacagawea's son, Jean-Baptiste. He called him "Pomp" for short.

When the group entered Shoshone country, Sacagawea was very helpful. She got her people to guide Lewis and Clark and to give them horses when needed. The history books all say that she was much more helpful on the trip than Charbonneau.

However, he never gave her one penny of the $500.33 that Lewis and Clark paid him for the job.

It is not known just when Sacagawea died, but she lived the rest of her life a poor woman. Perhaps knowing that Lewis and Clark were ever thankful for her help made her last years somewhat happier. Today there is a mountain top, a pass, and a river named after Sacagawea, to honor that brave woman.

2. Number the events to show the correct sequence.
   a. _____ Sacagawea got her people to guide Lewis and Clark and give them horses when needed.
   b. _____ The group entered Shoshone country.
   c. _____ Sacagawea had a mountain top, a pass, and a river named after her.
   d. _____ Sacagawea did not get paid.
   e. _____ The trip across the Rocky Mountains began.
   f. _____ Sacagawea died.

Check your answers with the key.

Doctors of the Old West

_____WORD STUDY_____

a. **bullet**   A piece of metal shot from a gun
b. **stomach**   The part of the body that holds food after the food has been swallowed
c. **surgery**   Operation done by a doctor to repair ailments or injuries

The doctor decided that (1) _____ was the only way to remove

the (2) _____ from the patient's (3) _____.

d. **wound**   An injury that results from cutting, tearing, or piercing of the skin and flesh
e. **examine**   To look at closely and carefully

Doctor, please (4) _____ the deep (5) _____ on my

finger.

f. **eyelid**   The piece of skin that moves to cover the eye
g. **pain**   The suffering caused by injury or sickness

I am in (6) _____ from the cut on my (7) _____.

h. **medicine**   A substance that is used to treat diseases
i. **health**   Being well or not sick

It is important to your (8) _____ to take your

(9) _____ daily.

_____START THE PLAYER_____

Proper Nouns

West	Dutch Kate	Dr. Charles Cole
Ezra Williams	Dr. Joseph McDowell	Dr. F. J. Bancroft
Dr. Thomas D. Hodges	Dr. Henry Hoyt	Dr. Sofie Herzog
California	Helena, Montana	Texas

DA-7

Doctors of the Old West

by Arthur Myers

Health and happiness was not always the lot of the people who won the West. It was dangerous country, made so by people and by nature. Fights and accidents were many. Doctors were few, and they had to make do with little in the way of medicines. But some of their adventures had a funny side, even though the people who actually lived them might not have thought so.

Answer questions 10 and 11.

▲10. This story will probably be about
  a. people who won the West.
  b. the way medicine helped people.
  c. some adventures of doctors in the Old West.
  d. how doctors brought happiness to people.

11. Which of the following statements are true? (Write or circle the letters of **all** correct choices.)
  a. There were many doctors in the Old West.
  b. Many people were hurt in fights and accidents.
  c. There were not many doctors in the Old West.
  d. Doctors did not have many kinds of medicine.

_____ **START THE PLAYER** _____

COMPREHENSION CHECK

Directions: Write or circle the letter of your choice.

12. Where did Dr. Thomas D. Hodges examine and work on Ezra Williams's wound?
    a. On a hospital bed
    b. In a bar
    c. In a hotel room
    d. At Williams's home

13. How did the crowd feel about Ezra's struggle with death?
    a. They were sad that Ezra might die.
    b. They were enjoying what was happening.
    c. It made them afraid.
    d. It made them angry.

14. Why did Dr. Joseph McDowell frighten his patients before doing surgery on them?
    a. He liked to yell loudly.
    b. He wanted to make them forget their pain.
    c. He wanted them to pay their bills on time.
    d. He was a mean man.

15. How did the miner pay Dr. Henry Hoyt for his help?
    a. He gave the doctor a $50 bill.
    b. He gave the doctor real gold.
    c. He didn't give the doctor anything.
    d. He gave the doctor gold that was not real.

▲16. Why was the robber so thankful to Dr. Charles Cole?
    a. Dr. Cole gave the robber his watch and money.
    b. Dr. Cole gave the robber a horse.
    c. Dr. Cole saved the robber's life.
    d. Dr. Cole shot the robber in the stomach.

▲17. Why would Dr. F. J. Bancroft have been the first to know if the man he was treating was about to die?
    a. The man would have told him.
    b. Nobody else in the room could see the man.
    c. The patient was hooked up to a breathing machine.
    d. Dr. Bancroft was a trained doctor.

18. What was one of Dr. Sofie Herzog's most prized possessions?
    a. A gun that a patient had given her
    b. Thousands of dollars in gold dust
    c. A necklace made of bullets
    d. Her bag of medicines

●19. This story is mainly about
    a. gold mining in California and Texas.
    b. the adventures of some doctors of the Old West.
    c. gunfighters of the Old West.
    d. the importance of surgery by doctors in the Old West.

Check your answers with the key.

START THE PLAYER

45

Health and happiness was not always the lot of the people who won the West. It was dangerous country, made so by people and by nature. Fights and accidents were many. Doctors were few, and they had to make do with little in the way of medicines. But some of their adventures had a funny side, even though the people who actually lived them might not have thought so.

Ezra Williams had been shot in a bar fight. He was lifted onto a pool table, and Dr. Thomas D. Hodges was called. As the doctor examined the wound, someone sang out, "I bet he dies."

"Fifty dollars he don't!" snapped the doctor.

It was a California gold mining camp, so there was plenty of ready money about, much of it in the form of gold dust. Before long, there was $14,600 riding on the idea that Ezra would not give up the ghost.

A bet of that amount could not fail to find takers in that country. For example, a very rich lady by the name of Dutch Kate put up $10,000 that Ezra would not last till morning.

Bottles in hand, the crowd sat comfortably watching Ezra's fight with death. They cheered his every groan, every flicker of his eyelid. Everyone was having a wonderful time—except Ezra.

At 2 o'clock in the morning he shivered into silence. The show seemed over. Cheerful shouts and gloomy groans filled the barroom. But Dr. Hodges was able to bring Ezra back. At 4 o'clock he almost died again. And again the doctor saved him—and, for the time being, his own $50. But at 5:30, Ezra had had it. He passed on to a better life. Thousands of dollars and gold dust changed hands, and everybody went home. It was just another night in the Old West.

20. Write the word *cause* or *effect*.

    a. _____ It was a California gold mining camp.

    b. _____ There was plenty of ready money about, much of it in the form of gold dust.

————START THE PLAYER————

21. Write the word *cause* or *effect*.

    a. _____ The crowd thought Ezra had died, and cheerful shouts and gloomy groans filled the bar room.

    b. _____ Ezra shivered into silence.

————START THE PLAYER————

22. Write the two effects of the following cause.

    Cause: At 5:30, Ezra passed on to a better life.

    Effect: _____

    Effect: _____

————START THE PLAYER————

•••• B ••••

When it came to surgery, there often was nothing to deaden the pain except for a shot of strong drink. So the doctor's way of handling things became very important. Dr. Joseph McDowell had a strange way of handling his patients. He would scare them into forgetting their pain.

"Where is that fellow?" he would shout in a loud, commanding voice as he entered the sickroom. "I have come to cut him to pieces! Why didn't he keep his silly leg away from that stupid saw?"

He would then wave his knife before the eyes of the frightened patient.

"Now hold still, sir," he would yell, "and I will make quick work of it!"

He would cut off the leg and dress the wound. Then in a gentle voice he would ask the man how he felt.

"Doctor," the patient would often reply, "you frightened me so badly I did not feel you cut my leg off at all."

23. Write the word **cause** or **effect**.

    a. _____ When it came to surgery, there often was nothing to deaden the pain.

    b. _____ The doctor's way of handling things became very important.

24. Write the word **cause** or **effect**.

    a. _____ The patients often did not feel any pain.

    b. _____ Dr. McDowell scared his patients.

_____START THE PLAYER_____

25. What caused Dr. McDowell's patients to become very frightened? (Write or circle the letters of **all** correct answers.)

    a. _____ Dr. McDowell would take a shot of strong drink before working on his patients.
    b. _____ Dr. McDowell would shout in a loud, commanding voice as he entered the sickroom.
    c. _____ They could feel the pain when the doctor operated.

    d. _____ Dr. McDowell would wave his knife before the eyes of his patients.
    e. _____ Dr. McDowell would always wear a scary costume.

_____START THE PLAYER_____

Then as now, there were plenty of thieves about. When Dr. Henry Hoyt worked on the badly shot-up arm of a miner, the man paid him in gold dust. When the doctor took the dust to the bank, he found it was not real gold. After that, he always tested the gold to make sure it was real.

One dark night in Helena, Montana, a robber demanded Dr. Charles Cole's watch and money. Cole refused, so the robber shot him in the arm. Cole pulled his gun and shot the robber in the stomach, after which, the man ran.

Soon someone came to the doctor's home, asking him to come to help a wounded man. The wounded man turned out to be the one Cole had shot. The doctor took his own bullet from the patient's stomach, and the man got well. The thankful robber took a job caring for the doctor's horses in order to pay his bill.

Doctors of the Old West had to be as ready as anyone else to defend themselves. One day a man shot in a gunfight was brought by his brother to Dr. F. J. Bancroft. The doctor examined the wound and said that the man's leg must come off. As a crowd gathered, the brother pulled a gun, waved it toward Bancroft, and announced he would shoot the doctor if the patient died.

Bancroft smiled and went calmly about his work. He succeeded. Later, one of the crowd asked him why he wasn't frightened.

"I, too, had a gun," the doctor replied, "and I would have been the first to know if the man was about to die."

There weren't many women doctors under those Western skies, but one was Sofie Herzog of Texas. When she went to her last resting place, one of her most prized possessions went with her. It was a necklace made of the bullets she had spent her life digging out of her wild and woolly patients of the Old West.

26. Write the word **cause** or **effect**.

    a. _____ At the bank, Dr. Hoyt found out that the dust was not real gold.

    b. _____ After that, Dr. Hoyt always tested the gold to make sure it was real.

27. What caused the robber to shoot Dr. Cole in the arm?
    a. Dr. Cole shot the robber first.
    b. Dr. Cole ran away.
    c. Dr. Cole refused to give the robber his watch and money.
    d. Dr. Cole had just robbed a bank.

28. What were the effects of Dr. Cole taking his own bullet from the robber's stomach? (Write or circle the letters of **all** correct answers.)
    a. The robber got well.
    b. The robber died during the night.
    c. The robber was put behind bars.
    d. The robber took all of Dr. Cole's money.
    e. The thankful robber took a job caring for the doctor's horses in order to pay his bill.

_____**START THE PLAYER**_____

PRACTICE

Reading for Cause and Effect

Directions: Read each section of the story. Then complete the exercises.

Savos Mikonos was very tired. He was the only one working in the bakery. Being the boss, he usually left at 3 P.M., and Betty—the woman who worked in the bakery every afternoon—stayed until closing. But Betty hadn't come in today because her son was very sick. That meant that Savos had to stay until closing time. To top it all off, it had been a very busy day, and at 72, Savos couldn't move as quickly as he once had.

"Maybe," Savos said to himself, "I am getting too old for this. My wife has been after me to sell the store, but what would I do without it? This bakery is my life."

1. Write the word *cause* or *effect*.

   a. _____ Betty's son was very sick.

   b. _____ Betty had to stay at home.

2. What caused Savos to be so tired? (Write or circle the letters of **all** your choices.)
   a. He was the only one working in the bakery.
   b. He couldn't go home at 3 P.M. as usual.
   c. He wanted to sell the store.
   d. It had been a very busy day.
   e. He was sick.
   f. He was 72 and couldn't move as quickly as he once had.

Savos was still talking to himself when he turned off the light in the store and went into the back room to clean up. His dinner would be waiting, and he was in a hurry to get home. Because he wasn't used to closing the bakery, he had to think about what needed to be done.

Suddenly he heard a noise in the store. Savos jumped up to look and saw a figure near the money box. He realized that not only had he left the door unlocked, but he had forgotten to take the money out of the money box. He went to the phone and quietly called the police. Savos was lucky: there was a police car nearby. The police, arriving just as the thief was leaving, caught him and saved Savos' money.

"I guess you'll think of selling the bakery now, Mr. Mikonos," the policewoman said.

"Not so," Savos answered. "I'll just remember to lock the door."

3. What were the effects of Savos not being used to closing the bakery? (Write or circle the letters of **all** your choices.)
   a. His dinner was waiting at home.
   b. He had to think about what needed to be done.
   c. He forgot to lock the door.
   d. The police caught the thief.
   e. He left the money in the money box.
   f. He didn't want to sell the bakery.

4. Write the word *cause* or *effect*.

   a. _____ The police caught the thief.

   b. _____ There was a police car nearby.

Check your answers with the key.

Making Comparisons

Two Creatures of the Past

_____WORD STUDY_____

a. **scores** — Great numbers
b. **ton** — A unit of weight equal to 2,000 pounds
c. **million** — One thousand thousands (1,000,000)
d. **dinosaur** — One of a group of extinct reptiles that lived millions of years ago. The dromaeosaurus and tyrannosaurus are two dinosaurs you will read about.

If you could go back in time over 65 (1) _____ years, you might

come face-to-face with a (2) _____ . There were

(3) _____ of these creatures walking the earth at that time, some

weighing more than a (4) _____ .

e. **area** — A particular space, region, or section
f. **pause** — To stop for a moment
g. **arrangement** — The act of putting in order

The (5) _____ of books in the library makes them easy to find.

Each (6) _____ of the library is clearly marked to let you know

what books you will find there. I always (7) _____ to think

about the kind of book I want to take out before heading for the shelves.

h. **perform** — To carry out or do
i. **talon** — A claw
j. **improve** — To make or become better

I always want to (8) _____ myself. Today I'm learning about

birds and the jobs the different parts of their body (9) _____ . For

example, an eagle uses its (10) _____ to kill other animals for food.

_____ START THE PLAYER _____

Proper Nouns

North America	Cretaceous

_____ **PREVIEW** _____
1. Read the title and look at the picture.
2. Read the first paragraph.
3. Then answer questions 11 and 12.
4. When you have finished, start the player.

Two Creatures of the Past
by Estelle Kleinman

People young and old have long been interested in dinosaurs. Since these creatures died out long before people came into being, we can only learn about them by studying their remains, usually the bones and teeth. Scientists have been able to learn more and more about these beasts as the means of collecting dinosaur remains improved, but they still don't have an easy job. The collection of dinosaur remains is very demanding in time and money. Even after bones have been carefully dug up and shipped, it takes many months to complete their arrangement to look like the dinosaur from which they came. Even so, remains of more than three hundred different kinds of dinosaurs have been found in all areas of the world. Two of these are the dromaeosaurus and the tyrannosaurus.

Answer questions 11 and 12.

11. Write the letters of **all** the things that are true about dinosaurs.
    a. We can only learn about them by studying their remains.
    b. They died out long before people came into being.
    c. They killed many people.
    d. Remains of more than three hundred dinosaurs have been found.
    e. Scientists have an easy job collecting their remains.

▲12. This story will probably be about
    a. the arrangement of dinosaur bones.
    b. two dinosaurs.
    c. why people are interested in dinosaurs.
    d. how scientists find dinosaur remains.

_____ **START THE PLAYER** _____

_____COMPREHENSION CHECK_____

Directions: Write or circle the letter of your choice.

13. The dromaeosaurus was a
    a. giant plant-eating dinosaur.
    b. giant meat-eating dinosaur.
    c. small plant-eating dinosaur.
    d. small meat-eating dinosaur.

14. Animals would have trouble getting away from a dromaeosaurus because it
    a. was very tall.
    b. could see very well and run very fast.
    c. had a good sense of smell.
    d. could hear very well and took very long steps.

▲15. From the story, you can tell that the dromaeosaurus was
    a. a cowardly creature.
    b. not very bright.
    c. a very good hunter.
    d. not able to defend itself.

16. A dromaeosaurus would have been more dangerous than a giant meat-eating dinosaur if it
    a. was very hungry.
    b. was guarding its young.
    c. hunted in packs.
    d. was sick.

17. The tyrannosaurus
    a. was the largest of the big meat-eating dinosaurs.
    b. was the oldest dinosaur to walk the earth.
    c. hunted with the dromaeosaurus.
    d. ruled the earth during the first 4 or 5 million years of Cretaceous times.

18. Why didn't the tyrannosaurus need speed?
    a. It had long, strong arms.
    b. It went after slow animals.
    c. It took very long steps.
    d. Other animals would bring it food.

19. Why did the tyrannosaurus have no trouble getting food?
    a. There were scores of giant plant-eating dinosaurs living nearby.
    b. It could eat plants as well as meat.
    c. It stored food in its stomach.
    d. There were scores of fish in the river.

●20. This story is mainly about
    a. how the dinosaurs disappeared at the end of the Cretaceous.
    b. how dinosaurs helped each other.
    c. how different dinosaurs hunted for food.
    d. what the dromaeosaurus and the tyrannosaurus were like.

Check your answers with the key.

_____ **START THE PLAYER** _____

People young and old have long been interested in dinosaurs. Since these creatures died out long before people came into being, we can only learn about them by studying their remains, usually the bones and teeth. Scientists have been able to learn more and more about these beasts as the means of collecting dinosaur remains improved, but they still don't have an easy job. The collection of dinosaur remains is very demanding in time and money. Even after bones have been carefully dug up and shipped, it takes many months to complete their arrangement to look like the dinosaur from which they came. Even so, remains of more than three hundred different kinds of dinosaurs have been found in all areas of the world. Two of these are the dromaeosaurus and the tyrannosaurus.

The dromaeosaurus was a meat-eating dinosaur that lived in North America during late Cretaceous times, about 65 to 100 million years ago. Next to the giant meat eaters of the time, the dromaeosaurus was quite small, being about 9 feet long from the tip of the nose to the end of the tail and 5 or 6 feet tall when standing upright. It weighed only about 100 pounds. Yet this small beast was a fierce killer. Its large eyes could see very well and quickly spotted a possible meal. Walking on two strong legs, the creature was very fast and had no trouble chasing game. Its head was 8 inches long and quite wide, and its mouth was lined with teeth as sharp as knives. On each foot was a 3-inch talon to cut open the stomach of a kill. All this would make even the bravest of creatures pause before crossing the path of a dromaeosaurus.

The neck of the dromaeosaurus was rather long, but thick and strong. The arms were very useful in catching and holding onto game. Each hand had three long fingers, which could grab almost anything. A long, stiff tail helped the dinosaur from falling when walking or running. Scientists believe that it may have hunted in packs or family groups. If so, this beast may have been even more dangerous than some of the giant meat-eating dinosaurs

like the tyrannosaurus.

The tyrannosaurus was the last of the giant meat-eating dinosaurs in North America, ruling the earth during the last several million years of late Cretaceous times. This largest known of the big meat eaters was about 50 feet from the tip of the nose to the end of the tail, and was 18½ feet tall when standing upright. It weighed anywhere from 6 to 8 tons. The huge head was more than 4 feet from front to back, and rested on a short, thick neck. The mouth was lined with knifelike teeth 6 inches long and 1 inch wide.

This giant creature was two-legged. Though it may have stood upright at times, it walked bent over with the giant tail stretched out to keep it from falling over. The tyrannosaurus was a very slow-moving dinosaur, not able to walk at much more than 3 miles an hour, less than the speed of a person walking. But this dinosaur didn't need speed because it took very long steps and had no trouble catching smaller, faster-moving animals. The tyrannosaurus had talons and used these as well as its mouth to catch and kill game. Being able to open its mouth very wide, this giant could swallow huge pieces of meat whole.

The tyrannosaurus could never have caught animals with its tiny arms. It is now thought that these arms, and the two-fingered hand at the end of each, performed the job of helping raise the dinosaur from the ground. When the animal was lying down with its legs folded, straightening the legs to lift the body would just serve to push the head and trunk along the ground. By using the sharp, hooked nails on its hands to stick to the ground, the tyrannosaurus stopped itself from sliding forward while rising.

Finding food was no trouble for this huge meat eater. There were scores of giant plant-eating dinosaurs living nearby. A tyrannosaurus would have no trouble attacking a 30-ton plant-eating dinosaur. This kill would give one tyrannosaurus enough food for three years.

Go on to the next page.

Dinosaurs, who walked the earth for 140 million years, vanished at the end of the Cretaceous. Nobody is certain why this happened, though scientists have come up with many ideas. One thing is certain—people will continue to study the dinosaurs through their remains. Perhaps one day we will have the answers to all our questions about these creatures from our past.

21. Complete the chart.	Dromaeosaurus	Tyrannosaurus
a. **Where it lived:**		
b. **When it lived:**		
c. **Length from nose to tail:**		
d. **How tall it was:**		
e. **Weight:**		
f. **Number of legs:**		
g. **Had talons (write *yes* or *no*):**		
h. **Speed (write *fast* or *slow*):**		
i. **Number of fingers on each hand:**		
j. **Use of arms and hands:**		

_____ **START THE PLAYER** _____

22. Which dinosaur was longer? _____

23. In what ways were the two dinosaurs alike? (Write or circle the letters of **all** your choices.)
    a. Where it lived
    b. When it lived
    c. How tall it was
    d. Weight
    e. Number of legs
    f. Had talons
    g. Speed
    h. Number of fingers on each hand

24. Which dinosaur weighed less? _____

25. Which dinosaur used its arms and hands while hunting? _____

26. Which dinosaur had fewer fingers? _____

27. Which dinosaur was slower? _____

_____ **START THE PLAYER** _____

PRACTICE
Making Comparisons

Directions: Read the story. Then complete the exercises.

Julia Goyle was in charge of filling job openings at the Progress Manufacturing Company. She liked her work because it gave her a chance to meet different kinds of people.

Last week Jed Wayne, who was 67 years old, had left the company, and his job was now open. So far Julia had seen eight people who wanted to fill that opening. Of the eight, Bob Peterson and Jackie Brown were best suited. Julia was having a very hard time making up her mind between the two of them.

Both Bob and Jackie had finished high school. As a matter of fact, both had done very well in school. They both appeared neat, but Bob seemed to be a better dresser. Julia knew that clothes didn't matter so much for the job, but she liked to see a well-dressed person.

When she checked their job histories, Julia found that Bob and Jackie both had good work habits and could be trusted to get the job done well. Jackie, with six years, had spent two more years than Bob doing the same kind of work for another company. Well, that certainly helped. Nevertheless, Bob's four years was long enough to show he, too, knew his job.

One thing that stood out in Julia's mind was that Jackie smiled a lot, while Bob seemed a bit edgy. Julia had felt very comfortable with Jackie and believed that anyone who worked with Jackie would probably feel the same way.

"I'm sure Bob can handle this job," Julia thought, "but Jackie is my first choice for this spot." Julia picked up the phone, called Jackie, and gave her the good news.

1. Complete the chart.

	Bob Peterson	**Jackie Brown**
a. **Finished high school (write *Yes* or *No*):**		
b. **Had good work habits (write *Yes* or *No*):**		
c. **Number of years at same kind of work:**		
d. **Smiled a lot (write *Yes* or *No*):**		

2. What did Bob and Jackie have in common? (Write or circle the letters of **all** your choices.)
    a. Finished high school
    b. Had good work habits
    c. Number of years at same kind of work
    d. Smiled a lot

3. Which one had spent more time at a job like the one open? _____

4. Which one was more likely to make people feel comfortable? _____

5. Which one got the job? _____

Check your answers with the key.

The *Sun* Takes a Look at the Moon

——WORD STUDY——

a. **report**   A detailed account about someone or something
b. **earthquake**   A shaking or trembling of the earth caused by forces far
                       below the earth's crust

Many people listened to their radios to hear the latest (1) _____

about the (2) _____.

c. **telescope**   A tubular magnifying instrument for viewing faraway ob-
                       jects such as stars and planets
d. **scientific**   Having to do with the methods or principles of science,
                       which is based on observed facts and tested truths

Some of the world's greatest (3) _____ discoveries about the uni-

verse were made with the help of the (4) _____.

e. **explode**   To break forth with a lot of force
f. **news**   Information about something that just happened
g. **newspaper**   Printed sheets of paper, published daily or weekly, with
                       information and stories about recent happenings

The (5) _____ of the war will probably (6) _____

across the front page of every (7) _____ in the country tomorrow.

h. **burst**   Suddenly give way to strong feelings
i. **hint**   To suggest instead of state outright
j. **customer**   A person who buys things

Dan's sister likes to (8) _____ about what she wants for a birthday

gift. That's how Dan knew that his sister wanted a brown hat. But when he

went to the store to buy one, another (9) _____ pushed ahead of

him in line. That made Dan mad enough to (10) _____.

——START THE PLAYER——

Proper Nouns

New York Sun	Cape of Good Hope	Yale University
United States	Africa	New Haven
Ben Day	Richard Locke	*Journal of Commerce*
Sir John Herschel	New York	

PREVIEW
1. Read the title and look at the picture.
2. Read the first two paragraphs.
3. Then answer questions 11 and 12.
4. When you have finished, start the player.

The *Sun* Takes a Look at the Moon

by Arthur Myers

In 1835, the *New York Sun* was only two years old, but it was a big baby. The *Sun* sold more papers than any other newspaper in the United States, 15,000 a day. This was a very large number for those times.

There were reasons for the paper's top place. For one thing, it sold for a penny, while the other newspapers in town cost six cents. It not only cost less than the other papers, it was livelier. The *Sun*'s writers never stopped looking for new ways to amaze and amuse the customers. The paper was full of startling stories. And the owner of the *Sun*, Ben Day, wasn't particular about how true they were.

Answer questions 11 and 12.

▲11. From the picture, you can tell that
a. the story takes place in 1980.
b. the newsboy is having trouble selling the newspapers.
c. many people want to read the newspaper.
d. the people find the news funny.

▲12. In this story, we will probably learn more about
a. the customers who read the newspaper.
b. what kind of person Ben Day was.
c. what price other newspapers sold for.
d. some of the stories in the *New York Sun*.

_____START THE PLAYER_____

_____COMPREHENSION CHECK_____

Directions: Write or circle the letter of your choice.

13. The story about Sir John Herschel's telescope
    a. was quite true.
    b. never appeared in the *Sun.*
    c. was about life on the moon.
    d. was not so truthful.

14. Richard Locke wrote his moon stories
    a. before Sir John Herschel set up a huge telescope.
    b. after the United States sent astronauts to the moon.
    c. after Sir John Herschel set up a huge telescope.
    d. while he was in his last year of high school.

15. Which of the following are true? (Write the letters of **all** correct answers.)
    a. No one read any of Locke's stories.
    b. Richard Locke made up the moon stories.
    c. The other papers were happy about how popular the *Sun* became.
    d. The *Sun* was forced to go out of business just after the moon stories came out.
    e. During the moon stories, the *Sun's* readers numbered as many as 19,000.

16. In the reports about life on the moon, Locke told about which of the following? (Write the letters of **all** correct choices.)
    a. Four-foot tall moonmen covered with red hair
    b. Horselike creatures with wings
    c. Blue, bearded creatures with single horns
    d. A beaverlike creature that walks on two feet
    e. Small, cowlike animals

    f. Bearded moonwomen that look like goats
    g. Ten-foot tall moonmen with short black hair
    h. Black and white birds with long legs and bills

▲17. Locke probably saved the moonmen story for last because he
    a. didn't want the other newspapers to know about the moonmen.
    b. didn't know what the moonmen looked like.
    c. wanted Ben Day to read the stories first.
    d. wanted to keep the people interested as long as possible.

18. One of Locke's friends
    a. planned to reprint the moon stories in another newspaper.
    b. was a professor who was interested in examining the scientific papers.
    c. was a scientist who saw the moonmen.
    d. wrote that the moon stories were true.

19. After the truth was known
    a. the *Sun* was never printed again.
    b. everyone stopped reading the *Sun.*
    c. the *Sun* lasted for another 115 years.
    d. the *Sun* printed only unpleasant news.

●20. This story is mainly about
    a. plant and animal life on the moon.
    b. how writers never tell the truth.
    c. how many readers in the 1830s believed some news stories about life on the moon.
    d. huge telescopes in Africa.

Check your answers with the key.

_____**START THE PLAYER**_____

●●●●A●●●●

In 1835, the *New York Sun* was only two years old, but it was a big baby. The *Sun* sold more papers than any other newspaper in the United States, 15,000 a day. This was a very large number for those times.

There were reasons for the paper's top place. For one thing, it sold for a penny, while the other newspapers in town cost six cents. It not only cost less than the other papers, it was livelier. The *Sun*'s writers never stopped looking for new ways to amaze and amuse the customers. The paper was full of startling stories. And the owner of the *Sun*, Ben Day, wasn't particular about how true they were.

One day a man by the name of Sir John Herschel set up a huge telescope at the Cape of Good Hope, which is found at the bottom tip of Africa. Sir John was a well-known scientist, and so the story was covered in many papers. The *Sun* was one of these papers. Even though this story was quite true, it started one of the *Sun*'s star writers, Richard Locke, thinking about a story that was not so truthful.

_____START THE PLAYER_____

21. Write the letters of **all** the main points from section A.
    a. In 1835, the *New York Sun* was the best selling newspaper in the United States because it cost very little and the stories were lively.
    b. The owner of the *Sun* was Ben Day.
    c. The *Sun*'s writers were always looking for new ways to amaze their readers.
    d. Sir John Herschel was an expert in the use of telescopes.
    e. A telescope was set up at the Cape of Good Hope in Africa.
    f. Many papers covered the story about the telescope.
    g. One of the *Sun*'s stories about a huge telescope in Africa gave writer Richard Locke the idea for some stories about life on the moon.

_____START THE PLAYER_____

•••• B ••••

A few days later, Locke wrote the first of several reports about life on the moon. He started off slowly, stating only that the new telescope had shown that there was life on the moon. The news hit New York like an earthquake. The next day, copies of the Sun were grabbed from the stands within minutes after they arrived. Locke was just warming up.

On the second day, August 26, he started off by telling about the different plants on the moon. Then he moved on to animal life. In a beautiful moon valley, Locke wrote, wandered large herds of small, cowlike animals. He also wrote about a pretty blue creature about the size of a goat. This fellow had a beard on its face and a single horn coming out of its head. Locke also threw in some big black and white birds with long legs and bills. He ended the story by hinting at even more fun in the next day's story—a creature that looked very much like a man!

By now the Sun's readers numbered more than 19,000 which made it the largest-selling newspaper in the world. The other New York papers were going out of their minds. Some were angry enough to burst. But others knew a good thing when they saw it. They started printing the Sun's moon stories.

On August 27, Locke wrote about the beautiful forests and wide plains of the moon. He also tossed in a beaverlike creature that walked on two feet, carried its young in its arms, and built small houses with smoke coming out of the chimneys. But, teasingly, he held off the moonmen.

By August 28, the mind of every New Yorker was on the moon. Locke now exploded the greatest discovery of all, the moonmen. These beings were about four feet tall, Locke wrote. They were covered, except for their faces, with short, red hair. Their faces looked something like those of monkeys, but smarter. They had large wings that folded neatly on their backs when they walked, and they waved their hands about when they talked. Locke stated that they walked and flew, but could they swim? Locke didn't make this quite clear. He did tell of a large lake, stating, "Some of these creatures had crossed this water and were lying like spread eagles on the edges of the wood." But Locke didn't tell how the creatures had crossed the lake.

22. Write the letters of **all** the main points from section B.
   a. Locke first wrote only that there was life on the moon, which was enough to catch the interest of the Sun's readers.
   b. Locke was just warming up.
   c. Locke next wrote about plant and animal life on the moon.
   d. He wrote about a pretty blue creature.
   e. He told about a valley on the moon.
   f. After the second moon story appeared, the Sun's readers grew to more than 19,000.
   g. Other papers either were angry or they joined in and reprinted the stories.
   h. Locke's last story told about the discovery of moonmen.
   i. The moonmen waved their hands about when they talked.

————START THE PLAYER————

•••• C ••••

Everyone seemed to have taken the stories quite seriously. And why not? Locke told his readers that his information came from certain scientific papers. A group of professors came down from Yale University to make an examination of these papers. There were no such papers, of course. The professors, shown in one door and out the other, returned to New Haven no wiser than before.

But then the great moon bubble burst. One of Locke's friends wrote for New York's most admired newspaper, the *Journal of Commerce*. This friend told Locke that the *Journal* was planning to reprint the moon stories. Not wanting his friend to look foolish, Locke told him that the stories weren't true. Locke's friend then wrote a piece exploding the whole thing.

The *Sun* rode with the waves, explaining that all it was trying to do was make fun of professors and amuse its readers. After all, the paper said, it was taking the people's minds off the unpleasant matters that usually made up the news.

The customers must have forgiven the *Sun*, for it lasted another 115 years.

23. Write the letters of **all** the main points from Section C.
   a. Everyone took the stories seriously.
   b. Yale professors came to New York from New Haven.
   c. Locke's friend wrote for the *Journal of Commerce*.
   d. When Locke's friend wanted to reprint the stories in his newspaper, Locke told him that the stories were untrue.
   e. Locke's friend wrote the truth.
   f. The *Sun* rode with the waves.
   g. People must have forgiven the *Sun* because it lasted another 115 years.

———— START THE PLAYER ————

Summary

In 1835, the *New York Sun* was the best selling newspaper in the United States because it cost very little and the stories were lively. The *Sun's* writers were always looking for new ways to amaze their readers. One of the *Sun's* stories about a huge telescope in Africa gave writer Richard Locke the idea for some stories about life on the moon.

Locke first wrote only that there was life on the moon, which was enough to catch the interest of the *Sun's* readers. Locke next wrote about plant and animal life on the moon. After the second moon story appeared, the *Sun's* readers grew to more than 19,000. Other newspapers either were angry or they joined in and reprinted the stories. Locke's last story told about the discovery of moonmen.

Everyone took the stories seriously. When Locke's friend wanted to reprint the stories in his newspaper, Locke told him that the stories were untrue. Locke's friend wrote the truth. People must have forgiven the *Sun* because it lasted another 115 years.

____PRACTICE____

Summarizing

Directions: Read the story. Then complete the exercise.

When I was ten, I lived in a small town in the Midwest. We didn't have any shows of our own, so visitors often came to town to amuse the people. One day a man named Mr. Bravisimo came to town and announced that he would put on a show that evening.

He set up a tent at the edge of town and got permission to use the church's chairs. My friends helped because Bravisimo promised that they could see the show for free. As for me, I had a special job. But you'll find out about that soon enough.

That evening everyone in town came. Nobody knew what would happen, but they were all sure it would be wonderful.

Bravisimo walked onto the stage carrying a large box that was open at the top and front. In it was a small farm scene with cows, horses, pigs, and a barn. He set the box down on a table. The bottom of the table was covered with a cloth.

"Ladies and gentlemen," he said, "I am here to amaze you with my voice. Watch this box carefully. Everytime I speak the animals will move. When I am silent, they will be still."

It really happened that way! He invited several people to the stage to try, but nobody could make the animals move. Just as my father's turn came, our dog ran into the tent and raced onto the stage. He bit into the cloth covering the table and raced away with it in his mouth. The box fell to the floor. There were little cows, horses, and pigs everywhere! At that moment everyone in town learned Bravisimo's secret. There I was, sitting under the now uncovered table. I was the one who was making those animals move only when Bravisimo spoke. The controls were under the table.

Do I have to tell you that Bravisimo left town sooner than expected? As for me, my father made sure that I couldn't sit down for a week!

1. Write or circle the letters of **all** the main points from the story.
   a. Mr. Bravisimo came to a small town to put on a show.
   b. He set up a tent at the edge of town and got permission to use the church's chairs.
   c. The storyteller's friends helped Bravisimo set up so they could see the show for free, but the storyteller had a special job.
   d. Nobody knew what would happen, but they were all sure it would be wonderful.
   e. Bravisimo brought a box on stage with a farm scene in it and placed it on a table covered with a cloth.
   f. The animals in the box moved only when Bravisimo spoke, but not when others spoke.
   g. When the storyteller's father tried to make the animals move, the family dog ran up on stage and raced off with the cloth.
   h. There were little cows, horses, and pigs everywhere.
   i. The storyteller was discovered sitting under the table and working the controls which caused the animals to move.

Check your answers with the key. Then read all the main points together to get a summary of the whole story.

Nothing Ever Changes

——WORD STUDY——

a. **flight** An airplane trip
b. **nineteen** A number [19] that is 9 more than 10
c. **protect** Keep from harm or danger

When I was (1) _____, I went on my first airplane

(2) _____. I carefully packed my mirror in my bag to

(3) _____ it from being broken.

d. **interrupt** Cut in while someone else is still talking
e. **suggest** Present an idea or possible way of acting

Please don't (4) _____ me while I'm speaking. I

(5) _____ that you wait until I'm finished.

f. **treat** Act toward
g. **protection** Anything that offers safety
h. **zero** A number [0] that is less than 1.

I (6) _____ my car well when it's below (7) _____

outdoors. One thing I do is keep it in the garage for (8) _____.

——START THE PLAYER——

Proper Nouns

Carol	Christmas
Florida	Vermont

_____PREVIEW_____
1. Read the title and look at the picture.
2. Read the first three paragraphs.
3. Then answer questions 9 and 10.
4. When you have finished, start the player.

Nothing Ever Changes

by Ali Reich

"Carol, are you listening to me?" called the voice from the other end of the phone.

"Yes, Mom," Carol answered, just barely hiding her anger. "But I still don't see why you can't come down here to Florida for the holidays. Every time I suggest it, you make some . . ."

"Don't be silly," her mother interrupted. "You know how I hate to fly. Besides, we might have snow for Christmas this year. There's nothing prettier than a white Christmas in Vermont. You'll come here, as usual."

Answer questions 9 and 10.

9. Carol lives
   a. in Florida.
   b. with her parents.
   c. in Vermont.
   d. somewhere between Florida and Vermont.

▲10. You can tell that Carol's mother
   a. is angry at her daughter.
   b. is listening carefully to what Carol is saying.
   c. expects Carol to do as she says.
   d. will go to Florida for Christmas.

_____START THE PLAYER_____

●●●●**A**●●●●

"Carol, are you listening to me?" called the voice from the other end of the phone.

"Yes, Mom," Carol answered, just barely hiding her anger. "But I still don't see why you can't come down here to Florida for the holidays. Every time I suggest it, you make some . . ."

"Don't be silly," her mother interrupted. "You know how I hate to fly. Besides, we might have snow for Christmas this year. There's nothing prettier than a white Christmas in Vermont. You'll come here, as usual."

As usual, Carol didn't push the point. Her mother told her what flight to take and what kind of clothes to bring. Carol listened without saying a word. When her mother had talked herself out, Carol said good-bye and hung up the receiver with such force that the cat ran under the table for protection.

"Why does she always do this to me?" Carol asked herself. "Why do I always give in?"

Carol looked at the calendar. In just nineteen days she would be back in the home she grew up in. Well, perhaps that was the fitting place to have it out with her mother once and for all.

———— START THE PLAYER ————

▲ 11. Why did Carol bang down the telephone?
    a. This was a usual game between her and her cat.
    b. She was angry because she had given in to her mother.
    c. She was in a hurry and dropped the receiver by accident.
    d. She was showing how excited she was about going home.

▲ 12. Carol probably feels that her mother treats her like
    a. a child.
    b. a grown-up.
    c. an enemy.
    d. a friend.

▲ 13. What kind of person is Carol's mother?
    a. Sweet
    b. Controlling
    c. Shy
    d. Weak

———— START THE PLAYER ————

•••B•••

Carol's flight was late. It had been snowing hard all day. "Mom's right again. We're going to have a white Christmas," she thought.

When she got off the plane, her father was waiting for her. He kissed her hello. Carol was shivering as they made their way to the car.

"I forgot how cold it gets here," she told her father. "It feels like it's below zero."

"Your mother sent along this coat for you. She figured you'd be cold. She thought . . ."

"I wouldn't have enough sense to bring a warm coat," Carol snapped.

Her father gave her a sharp look. "Your mother means well."

"That's not the point, Dad. She's got to realize that I'm not a child anymore."

"Please don't say anything. Not now," her father begged.

He sounded so troubled that Carol was a little taken by surprise. She decided not to talk to her father about it anymore. But if her mother got her angry, this time she was going to let her mother know how she felt.

_____START THE PLAYER_____

▲ 14. How does Carol probably feel when her mother turns out to be right about having snow for Christmas?
- a. Very frightened
- b. Somewhat thankful
- c. Very amused
- d. Slightly bothered

▲ 15. Carol probably finds her father
- a. easier to talk to than her mother.
- b. harder to talk to than her mother.
- c. as hard to talk to as her mother.
- d. more maddening to talk to than her mother.

▲ 16. Why did Carol stop talking to her father about her mother?
- a. She was afraid that he would tell her mother.
- b. She was angry at him and didn't want to talk to him anymore.
- c. She had nothing more to say.
- d. She didn't want to upset him.

_____START THE PLAYER_____

•••C•••

As soon as Carol walked into the house, a warm feeling came over her. Everything looked the same.

"Is that you, Carol? Come in here," her mother called from the kitchen.

"Giving orders already," Carol thought. But she walked into the kitchen. Nothing had changed but the year on the calendar hanging on the wall. Well, maybe one thing had changed. Her mother looked a little paler than usual.

"Hi, dear," her mother said. "I knew you'd be hungry so I prepared something for you to eat."

"I'm not hungry, Mom. I ate on the plane."

"Of course you're hungry. The food they give on airplanes isn't fit to eat. Here, have some of . . ."

"I said I ate on the plane," Carol said with

such force that it surprised even her.

"Well, you don't have to shout. I can hear you."

"I wonder if you ever hear me. I talk, but you don't listen." Carol had started and she couldn't stop. Not even the warning look from her father was able to calm her down.

"What do you mean?" her mother asked in a hurt voice.

"You've got to stop treating me like a child. I'm a woman. I have a good job and I take good care of myself. If you'd just come down to visit, you'd . . ."

"So that's what this is all about," her mother interrupted. "You're mad because I didn't want to go to Florida."

"And why didn't you come? Are you afraid to see how well I can get along without you? That I don't need you to protect me?"

"That's enough," Carol's father broke in with a commanding voice. "Come with me, Carol. Now."

Carol had mixed feelings. She wanted to finish the fight with her mother, but she was almost glad that her father had stopped it.

Carol walked outside with her father. As they walked along, her father put his arm around her.

"There's something I should tell you," he said in a sad voice. "Your mother has a serious bone disease, and there's no cure for it. Possibly, she has six months to live."

Carol swallowed hard. So this was the final family Christmas. Nothing would be quite the same again.

Carol ran back to the house. Her mother was sitting in the big easy chair.

"Mom, I'm sorry. I . . ."

"I'm sorry, too. I've been thinking things over. I do treat you like a child sometimes. I guess to me you'll always be my little girl. I'll try to watch what I say from now on. And I would like to see your home in Florida. Next year, we'll come to you for Christmas."

"Yes, next year." Carol bit her lip to hold back the tears.

▲ 17. Why did Carol have a warm feeling when she entered the house?
   a. She'd just had a bowl of very hot soup.
   b. She probably remembered the many happy times she had there while she was growing up.
   c. She hadn't yet taken off her heavy winter coat.
   d. The heat from the fireplace made the house too warm.

▲ 18. Why did Carol speak so fiercely when she said she wasn't hungry?
   a. She knew her parents were poor and didn't want to eat all their food.
   b. She really was hungry but didn't want anyone to know.
   c. All the angry feelings she held toward her mother were finally coming out.
   d. She hated her mother's cooking more than anything in the world.

▲ 19. Why did Carol have mixed feelings about her father stopping the fight?
   a. She was afraid that she would lose the fight to her mother.
   b. She wanted to win the fight but did not want to hurt her mother.
   c. She hoped her father would do the fighting for her.
   d. She wanted to hurt her mother but didn't want her father to know it.

▲ 20. How did Carol feel after her father told her that her mother was going to die?
   a. Sad and sorry
   b. Happy and excited
   c. Cold and hungry
   d. Calm and tired

▲ 21. From what Carol's mother said about going to Florida next year, we can guess that Carol's mother
   a. really loves to fly, especially to sunny places.
   b. will live longer than the doctors said.
   c. doesn't know she will soon die.
   d. will never change her way of treating Carol.

_____ **START THE PLAYER** _____

_____COMPREHENSION CHECK_____

Directions: Write or circle the letter of your choice.

22. On the telephone, Carol and her mother had a fight over
    a. what Carol should wear.
    b. where Carol lived.
    c. where they should spend Christmas.
    d. what they should have for dinner.

23. Carol gave in to her mother this time, but decided
    a. never to speak again to her mother.
    b. not to bring her parents any Christmas gifts.
    c. to bring all her friends to Vermont with her.
    d. to stand up to her mother the next time.

▲24. Carol's father didn't want Carol to argue with her mother because he
    a. knew his wife was going to die.
    b. was afraid his wife would hit Carol.
    c. thought fighting would make Carol sick.
    d. wanted to argue with his wife himself.

25. Shortly after Carol walked into the house, she had a fight with her mother in which she complained that her mother
    a. never cooked for her.
    b. treated her like a child.
    c. didn't love her.
    d. always shouted at her.

▲26. Why did Carol's father stop the fight?
    a. He was sick and tired of the noise.
    b. He didn't want Carol to be sorry later.
    c. He felt left out and was angry with both Carol and her mother.
    d. He wanted Carol to help him set up the Christmas tree.

27. Carol's mother had a
    a. bad headache from the fight.
    b. broken bone from a fall.
    c. burned hand from a cooking accident.
    d. disease for which there was no cure.

▲28. By the way Carol and her mother act at the end of the story, you can tell that they
    a. both hated snow.
    b. really loved each other.
    c. lived in the same town.
    d. were angry with Carol's father.

●29. This story is mainly about
    a. what it is like to spend a snowy Christmas in Vermont.
    b. why a woman is afraid of airplane flights.
    c. how a mother and daughter come to new understandings about each other.
    d. a man who loves his wife more than he loves his daughter.

Check your answers with the key.

Go on to the next page.

PRACTICE

Making Inferences

Directions: Read each part of the story. Then answer the questions by writing or circling the letter of your choice.

When Mickey Morales was a boy, he got what he wanted by fighting. Now he fought for a living. Although Mickey usually won his fights, he didn't often bother to practice his footwork or his timing. Why should he? He could hit hard. And he was fast. Fast— and lucky.

Ralph, his manger and trainer, often tried to get Mickey to practice his boxing. But Mickey always said, "Oh yeah? When was the last time you won a fight?"

▲ 1. Mickey is
   a. kind and sweet.
   b. shy and serious.
   c. hardworking and patient.
   d. boastful and too sure of himself.

Ralph was the only friend Mickey had. He was there no matter how Mickey treated him. He figured Mickey needed at least one true friend.

Ralph worked hard to get Mickey a chance to fight the champion. He kept telling Mickey to train seriously, but Mickey refused. "Listen," Mickey said, "I fought him when we were both in the army and won. I'll win again."

Ralph shook his head. "If he'd only listen to me."

▲ 2. Ralph felt that Mickey
   a. would now start listening to him.
   b. was going to lose the fight.
   c. treated him well.
   d. would win the fight.

The night of the fight, Mickey told everyone that he would be the next champion. "He's a pushover. I licked him once, and I can do it again."

In the ring it was a different story. The champion came in hitting hard and fast. He kept out of Mickey's way with fine footwork. His timing was beautiful. Toward the end of the second round, the champ knocked Mickey down. The fight was over. Mickey had lost.

Mickey told all the reporters that it was Ralph's fault that he'd lost. Ralph shook his head sadly. "Kid," he said, "maybe one day you'll learn what it takes to become a champ. But if you do, it'll be without me. Find yourself another trainer, kid. I quit."

▲3. Mickey is a person who
   a. isn't afraid to admit he was wrong.
   b. cannot face losing.
   c. learns from his mistakes.
   d. knows he needs a friend.

▲4. Ralph quit as Mickey's manager and trainer because he
   a. has had enough of Mickey's excuses.
   b. knows he doesn't know how to train.
   c. became friends with the champion.
   d. stays friends only with winners.

Check your answers with the key.

——WORD STUDY——

a.	**claws**	Sharp, curved nails on the foot of an animal
b.	**difficult**	Hard or not easy
c.	**tame**	Gentle or not wild
d.	**weary**	Very tired

Lions are dangerous animals with long (1) _____. Few lions ever

become really (2) _____, so they are (3) _____ to

train. It is no wonder that lion trainers get (4) _____ after working

all day with these wild animals.

e.	**insist**	Take a stand and refuse to give in
f.	**steady**	Regular or even
g.	**helmet**	A protective covering for the head

A riding teacher will always (5) _____ that a person wear a

(6) _____ during a riding lesson. A beginner will be put on a

quiet horse that has a slow, (7) _____ way of moving.

h.	**human**	A person
i.	**gravity**	The planetary force that pulls things toward the ground

Because of the low (8) _____ on the moon, the three astronauts

weighed less than 50 pounds each. They couldn't help being excited—no

(9) _____ had ever set foot on the moon before.

——START THE PLAYER——

Proper Nouns

London	Aldershot	Liverpool
Jane Alsop	John Regan	
Jumping Man	Newport	

_____PREVIEW_____
1. Read the title and look at the picture.
2. Read the first paragraph.
3. Then answer questions 10 and 11.
4. When you have finished, start the player.

The Jumping Man

by Arthur Myers

One evening, in 1837, a young London woman named Jane Alsop heard the bell ringing on the gate in front of her house. She went to the door and saw a tall figure standing on the porch. She held a lighted candle toward him. With a roar, he fell back and threw off a long coat. The young woman stood frozen at the sight she saw.

Answer questions 10 and 11.

▲10. Jane Alsop saw something that
    a. made her angry.
    b. made her happy.
    c. frightened her.
    d. made her sad.

▲11. This story will probably tell us more about
    a. the tall figure that Jane saw.
    b. life in London today.
    c. Jane's house.
    d. Jane's candles.

_____START THE PLAYER_____

COMPREHENSION CHECK

Directions: Write or circle the letter of your choice.

12. When Jane Alsop held a lighted candle toward the Jumping Man, he
    a. smiled at her.
    b. threw off a long coat.
    c. turned to ice.
    d. spoke to her.

▲13. Why did Jane Alsop freeze at the sight of the Jumping Man?
    a. He looked very strange.
    b. She thought his clothes were too dirty.
    c. She thought that he had died many years earlier.
    d. She recognized him.

▲14. When the two army men saw that gunfire didn't harm the Jumping Man, they were probably
    a. happy.
    b. surprised.
    c. tired.
    d. lonely.

▲15. If the strange man seen in Liverpool was the same Jumping Man that Jane Alsop saw, the Jumping Man must have been
    a. around for only a short time.
    b. seen more than 23 times in four years.
    c. around for 67 years or more.
    d. very young the last time he was seen.

16. Write the letters of **all** the things that the Jumping Man could do.
    a. Burn down buildings
    b. Be shot with a gun and not be harmed
    c. Perform card tricks
    d. Jump as high as 30 feet
    e. Blow blue flames through an opening in his head covering

▲17. Why did so many people in Liverpool gather to look at the Jumping Man?
    a. They were tired.
    b. They were curious.
    c. They were hungry.
    d. They were forgetful.

18. How does the writer explain who or what the Jumping Man was?
    a. The writer tells us that the Jumping Man came from the moon.
    b. The writer tells us that the Jumping Man was really a woman.
    c. The writer tells us that the Jumping Man was never real because the story is only make-believe.
    d. The writer tells us that the Jumping Man might have come from another planet.

●19. The story is mainly about
    a. someone in London dressed up in a frightening costume.
    b. a strange jumping creature seen by many people during the 1800s and the beginning of the 1900s.
    c. life on other planets.
    d. people in England who like to make up funny stories.

Check your answers with the key.

START THE PLAYER

••••A••••

Setting 1

One evening, in 1837, a young London woman named Jane Alsop heard the bell ringing on the gate in front of her house. She went to the door and saw a tall figure standing on the porch. She held a lighted candle toward him. With a roar, he fell back and threw off a long coat. The young woman stood frozen at the sight she saw.

He was wearing what seemed to be a white, smooth, close-fitting suit. His head was enveloped in a round covering that looked like a modern astronaut's helmet. His arms ended in claws. Miss Alsop insisted she could see two angry eyes inside the helmet.

Already in terror, she was even more horrified when the creature jumped toward her. He was breathing blue-white flames through an opening in the front of his head covering. Her sister heard her screams and came running, and this seemed to scare off the creature. He went running off into the night.

End setting 1

The police looked on Miss Alsop's story as a tall one indeed, until a young man came to them with the same report. Several days before, he said, his two sisters had been attacked. When they screamed, the creature took flight and jumped over a brick wall. This wall was over fourteen feet high! This was another difficult story to believe, but many people did. The newspapers called the creature the "Jumping Man."

Setting 2

For eight years, nothing more was heard from him. Then a steady flow of new reports began to come in. The Jumping Man was seen flying over fences and walls in different parts of London. Then he disappeared again.

———START THE PLAYER———

Setting 1
20. When does it take place? _____

———START THE PLAYER———

21. Where does it take place? _____

———START THE PLAYER———

Setting 2
22. When does it take place? _____

23. Where does it take place? _____

———START THE PLAYER———

••••**B**••••

Setting 3 ☛

In the 1860s and 1870s the Jumping Man showed up in the country. He would come soaring over a wall and land noiselessly in front of somebody on a country road. Then, with another great jump, he would soar back over the wall and vanish completely. Understandably, nobody tried to catch him, even though he seemed tame enough. He never did any real damage or hurt anyone.

Setting 4 ☛

Just a lot of wild stories, the police insisted. But one summer day in 1877, the Jumping Man put in an appearance that was hard to argue away. At an army post near Aldershot, a guard named John Regan said he suddenly felt a cold breath on his cheek. He screamed and dropped his gun. Another guard came running. As they stood there, a large, dark shape passed over them and landed without a sound not far away. Then the strange figure straightened up and stood quietly, a shining "bubble" over its head. The guard who still was carrying his gun aimed and fired. All that happened was that the Jumping Man jumped toward and then over the two men, blowing blue flames from its bubble. Now both guards were firing their guns at the Jumping Man, but they couldn't harm him. Again the strange creature vanished.

Setting 3

24. When does it take place? _____

25. Where does it take place? _____

Setting 4

26. When does it take place? _____

27. Where does it take place? _____

_____START THE PLAYER_____

●●●●C●●●●

Setting 5 ☛

Four months later, in the town of Newport, the Jumping Man was spotted on the roof of a house. He stood there for some time, and many people got a good look at him. It was noticed this time that he had long, pointed ears. When someone shouted, the creature jumped over the heads of the crowd and appeared some minutes later on top of one of Newport's larger buildings. An expert shot fired at him, but again the creature remained unhurt. After a while, he took off again with 20-foot-high jumps.

Setting 6 ☛

During the years that followed, the Jumping Man was seen again and again. But in 1904 he made his last, and greatest, appearance. He appeared in Liverpool in the middle of the day, and hundreds of people saw him. He performed—and "performed" seems to be the right word— for a full ten minutes.

He jumped up and down the streets and easily over houses. He seemed to be having great fun—putting on a joyful show. And then, it seems, he grew weary of the show. He vanished—this time for good.

End setting 6 ☚

The question of who—or what—he was has never been answered. He certainly was not an animal, for he was shaped too much like a human. But no human being could possibly make jumps as high as 30 feet!

Perhaps time is giving us some answers to the mystery. The suits of the astronauts who jumped about in the low gravity of the moon look a lot like that worn by the Jumping Man. He seems to have been breathing some sort of gas inside his head bubble. When he blew it out, the gas mixed with the earth's air to form a harmless blue-white flame.

All in all, it might well seem that the Jumping Man was a visitor from somewhere else in space. Perhaps he was just taking a look at the strange forms of life on our little planet.

Setting 5

28. When does it take place? _____

29. Where does it take place? _____

Setting 6

30. When does it take place? _____

31. Where does it take place? _____

_____START THE PLAYER_____

PRACTICE

Understanding Setting

Directions: Read each section of the story. Then answer the questions.

It was a quiet afternoon in the newsroom of the *New City News*. Amy had just finished looking over her story when she saw her boss walking toward her at full speed.

"Amy, there's a fire out of control on Main Street," he said quickly. "So far two buildings are down, and we don't know how many lives lost. Get down there! Keep calling us as the story develops. Jake will go along to take pictures."

1. When does this section take place? _____

2. Where does this section take place? _____

When Amy and Jake arrived at Main Street, they could hardly believe their eyes. There had never been a fire of this size in the history of New City. Even though it was winter, the heat from the fire was so great that they didn't need their coats.

Since they had left the office, one more building had burned down. Twelve people had died, and many others were being brought to the hospital.

Amy questioned some of the people at the scene about how the fire started while Jake took pictures. In order to get good pictures, Jake was moving closer and closer to the burning buildings. Suddenly the wall of one fell, and hit Jake. A group of firefighters dug Jake out and had him rushed to the hospital.

3. When does this section take place? _____

4. Where does this section take place? _____

Amy arrived at the hospital a little while after Jake had. Searching for Jake, she walked down the halls lined with people who had been hurt. There were so many to take care of that doctors had been called in from other hospitals.

When she looked at her watch, Amy saw that it was almost morning. Even though it had been many hours since the fire had started, people were still being brought to the hospital.

Amy found Jake sitting up in a chair. Luckily, he wasn't badly hurt. It was then that Amy realized that she had been so worried about Jake that she had forgotten to call in. Amy ran to the nearest phone and called the newsroom. "Boy, do I have a story for you!" she exclaimed to the voice that answered the phone.

5. When does this section take place? _____

6. Where does this section take place? _____

Check your answers with the key.

Her Highness

____WORD STUDY____

a. **court** — The place where trials are held
b. **freedom** — Being physically free to go and do as you please
c. **jail** — A building in which criminals are locked up
d. **nervous** — Anxious or upset

Frank was (1) _____ as he was brought into

(2) _____. If the judge decided to send him to

(3) _____, Frank could lose his (4) _____ for five

years.

e. **accuse** — Charge someone with wrongdoing
f. **fist** — A firmly closed hand, with the fingernails touching the palm
g. **suspect** — A person believed to be guilty of a crime

The man shook his (5) _____ at the (6) _____ and

screamed, "I (7) _____ you of robbing my store."

h. **dignity** — Quality of character that wins the respect and high opinion of others
i. **shove** — Push
j. **uneasy** — Uncomfortable

Martha always felt (8) _____ in a crowded elevator. She often had

to (9) _____ her way out—an act she felt was below her

(10) _____.

____START THE PLAYER____

Proper Nouns

Judge Iris Green	Mr. Simmons

_____PREVIEW_____
1. Read the title and look at the picture.
2. Read the first paragraph.
3. Then answer questions 11 and 12.
4. When you have finished, start the player.

Her Highness

by Sarah Lang

Judge Green's first name was Iris, but nobody at court ever called her that, even behind her back. When people did talk about her out of her hearing, they called Judge Green "Her Highness." That was because the judge acted more like a queen than a judge. She always kept her head held high and spoke in a loud voice as if she were addressing a whole nation, not just a courtroom. Above all, Judge Green prized her dignity. She had made it clear on her first day in court that no one was ever to call her Iris, or talk to her about private matters. Judge Green was all business.

Answer questions 11 and 12.

11. What did people call Judge Green behind her back?
    a. Iris
    b. Queen
    c. Her Highness
    d. Ms. Green

12. Write the letters of **all** the things that are true about Judge Green.
    a. She likes to talk about her private life.
    b. She always keeps her head held high.
    c. She speaks in a loud voice.
    d. She acts very shy.
    e. She is all business.

_____START THE PLAYER_____

——COMPREHENSION CHECK——

Directions: Write or circle the letter of your choice.

13. Judge Green believed in
    a. sending all lawbreakers to jail.
    b. not sending young lawbreakers to jail.
    c. being easy on all lawbreakers.
    d. being harder on teenage law-breakers than on grown-ups.

14. The subway train Judge Green got on was
    a. very comfortable.
    b. hot and crowded.
    c. cold.
    d. empty.

15. What happened to the train?
    a. It crashed into another train.
    b. It went past Judge Green's stop.
    c. It fell off the tracks.
    d. It got stuck between stations.

16. On the train, Judge Green met
    a. her uncle.
    b. her former homeroom teacher.
    c. her best friend.
    d. a man whom she had sent to jail.

17. Mr. Simmons remembered the time when Judge Green had
    a. helped another student with his work.
    b. studied hard to pass a history test.
    c. hit a boy because he'd called her dumb.
    d. fallen and broken her nose.

▲18. When Iris Green told Mr. Simmons she was a judge, he was
    a. not at all surprised.
    b. frightened.
    c. mad.
    d. somewhat surprised.

19. That day in court, Judge Green
    a. sent many people to jail.
    b. didn't send anyone to jail.
    c. took sick and went home.
    d. told everyone to call her "Iris."

●20. This story is mainly about
    a. what to do when a subway train breaks down.
    b. a teacher who took an interest in one of his former students.
    c. what happens in a court of law.
    d. a judge who was hard on law-breakers because of her past.

Check your answers with the key.

——START THE PLAYER——

Judge Green's first name was Iris, but nobody at court ever called her that, even behind her back. When people did talk about her out of her hearing, they called Judge Green "Her Highness." That was because the judge acted more like a queen than a judge. She always kept her head held high and spoke in a loud voice as if she were addressing a whole nation, not just a courtroom. Above all, Judge Green prized her dignity. She had made it clear on her first day in court that no one was ever to call her Iris, or talk to her about private matters. Judge Green was all business.

Today, as the judge left her house and walked to the subway, she thought about the day ahead. It would be the usual round of suspects, people accused of small robberies or fights. As usual, she would probably send most of the people to jail for some time. Judge Green didn't believe in giving freedom to lawbreakers, even young ones. As a teenager, Judge Green had gotten into a lot of trouble, trouble that might never have happened if someone had been tougher on her. It was a time she didn't like to remember.

———————START THE PLAYER———————

▲ 21. Judge Green seems to be
    a. very proud.
    b. happy.
    c. careless.
    d. stupid.

———————START THE PLAYER———————

▲ 22. Judge Green
    a. likes everybody she meets.
    b. does not like her job.
    c. thinks that other people are better than she is.
    d. does not let people get close to her.

———————START THE PLAYER———————

▲ 23. How does Judge Green feel about her teenage years?
    a. She is happy about them and likes to think about them often.
    b. She is so uncomfortable about them that she doesn't want to remember them.
    c. She is amused when she thinks about the trouble she used to get into.
    d. She is frightened by them because she might start getting into trouble again.

24. Why does Judge Green think she got into trouble as a teenager?
    a. She was in with a bad crowd.
    b. Nobody had been tough on her.
    c. Her parents didn't love her.
    d. Her teachers took no interest in her.

25. What kind of judge is she?
    a. A stupid one   c. An easy one
    b. A funny one   d. A tough one

———————START THE PLAYER———————

●●●●B●●●●

There was a large crowd on the subway platform, and it was very hot. Well, it would be an unpleasant ride today, for sure. Though crowds made Judge Green uneasy, she put up with them in order to get to work. Once in the courtroom, she would forget the people shoving to get on the train, forget the heat. For in the courtroom, Iris Green stood above the crowd. She was "Your Honor." The first time anyone had called her "Your Honor," Iris Green knew she had left her difficult past behind and had become someone important.

A train pulled into the station, and everyone rushed to get on it. The heat and all the people standing so close to her made her nervous. The judge felt sorry she hadn't waited for a less crowded train.

Worst of all, the train slowed down and then stopped in between stations. Soon, an announcement was made that the train couldn't move because of trouble on the tracks. The judge's whole car fell silent at this news. People looked at one another unhappily, knowing they would probably have a long wait.

26. How does Judge Green feel in crowds?
    a. Happy
    b. Sad
    c. Uneasy
    d. Amused

27. How does Judge Green feel when she is in the courtroom?
    a. Scared
    b. Sad
    c. Dumb
    d. Important

▲ 28. Judge Green thinks that she is
    a. better than other people.
    b. not as good as other people.
    c. happier than other people.
    d. sadder then other people.

———START THE PLAYER———

Suddenly, a loud but shaky voice broke the silence with the words, "Iris Green!" The judge looked around in surprise. Standing to her left was an old, white-haired man. At first Judge Green didn't recognize him. But as she looked more closely, she realized that he was Mr. Simmons, her homeroom teacher for two years in high school.

"Hello, Mr. Simmons," Judge Green said.

"I'm sorry, but you'll have to speak louder," shouted Mr. Simmons. "I'm a little hard of hearing now, you see."

Judge Green did see, and wished she were somewhere else. She wanted to be anywhere but in this place. She felt that all the people trapped in the subway car were listening to her talk to her old high school teacher.

"I wasn't sure for a minute there whether it was you," Mr. Simmons said. "It's been so many years. But I guess I could never really forget Iris."

Hearing this, a couple of people in the car laughed. Everyone else looked on curiously. Judge Green felt as if she were fifteen years old again and prayed for the train to take off. She said, "I've changed a lot since high school, Mr. Simmons—for the better, I'm sure."

"Well, I'm glad to hear that, Iris," Mr. Simmons said. "I've often thought about what might have become of you. I never saw a girl with so much anger. The littlest things would set you off. Do you remember the time you started a fight with that boy who sat next to you, because he said you were dumb? You hit him right in the nose. I always said that you'd either end up in jail or be somebody famous."

"I'm a judge now, Mr. Simmons," Iris Green said. She thought about the years she'd spent in law school, and the years of hard work afterwards, proving she wasn't dumb. No one would ever be able to call her that again.

"A judge, of all things," Mr. Simmons said. "You have come a long way. You know, you never were exactly the smartest kid in the class." Mr. Simmons chuckled, and a few other people in the car chuckled with him. Iris Green made a fist. At that moment the train took off again. "Thank goodness Mr. Simmons is not trying to talk above the noise," Judge Green thought. When the train stopped at her station, she hurried off.

That day in court, Judge Green set a record for the number of people sent to jail in one day.

▲29. How does Iris feel when Mr. Simmons brings up her past?
  a. Happy
  b. Uncomfortable
  c. Thankful
  d. Old

30. Mr. Simmons says that Iris was
  a. a good student.
  b. a kind person.
  c. an angry girl.
  d. his friend.

▲31. Why do you think Iris became a judge?
  a. She wanted to prove her worth to others.
  b. She liked the law.
  c. She couldn't think of anything else to do.
  d. Her father had been a judge.

▲32. Why do you think Judge Green sent so many people to jail that day?
  a. She didn't like them.
  b. They wanted to go.
  c. She wanted to show her power.
  d. She wanted to set a record.

____PRACTICE____
Understanding Character and Feelings

Directions: Read the story. Then answer each question by writing or circling the letter of your choice.

Jessie had been lucky when she'd answered Mrs. Mitchell's ad. Not only did she get the job as the new cleaning woman, but Jessie was also trusted enough to be left alone in the apartment.

Jessie really needed this job. Her husband had walked out on her and their little girl over a month ago. Now it was up to her to support herself and her child.

As Jessie was cleaning, she noticed a beautiful blue cup sitting on the shelf. It was so pretty that she couldn't stop herself from picking it up.

Behind her the doorbell rang. The sudden ring startled her, and the cup fell from her hands. It lay in pieces on the floor.

After a long moment, Jessie answered the door. A boy shoved a package at her. She signed for it with shaking hands, and the boy left.

What would she tell Mrs. Mitchell? Perhaps she could make up a story. She could say....The boy! That was it! He broke the cup.

When she heard a key in the lock, Jessie jumped. Mrs. Mitchell came in. When Jessie was face to face with Mrs. Mitchell, she decided to tell Mrs. Mitchell the truth.

Jessie had finished her story, but Mrs. Mitchell only stared at her. Jessie looked very frightened.

"Don't worry, Jessie," Mrs. Mitchell finally said. "The cup was just something I picked up in a second-hand shop. Forget about it. Now, can you come back next week?"

"Yes," was all Jessie could answer. As she left, there was a loud singing in her heart.

After the door closed, Mrs. Mitchell looked at the broken cup. It had been her grandmother's, and she had loved it. Why hadn't she told this to Jessie? Perhaps because her grandmother had been the kindest person she had ever known. She would never allow her grandmother's lovely cup to hurt anyone.

▲ 1. How does Jessie feel when she breaks the cup?
a. Happy
b. Uncaring
c. Very frightened
d. Somewhat amused

▲ 2. What kind of person is Jessie?
a. Brave and truthful
b. Mean and tricky
c. Silly and stupid
d. Impatient and uncaring

▲ 3. How does Mrs. Mitchell feel when Jessie tells her the cup is broken?
a. Happy
b. Frightened
c. Angry
d. Sad

▲ 4. How does Jessie feel when Mrs. Mitchell tells her to forget about the cup?
a. Sad
b. Happy
c. Frightened
d. Angry

▲ 5. What kind of person is Mrs. Mitchell?
a. Selfish
b. Unfeeling
c. Kind
d. Silly

Check your answers with the key.

——WORD STUDY——

a. **dull**   Not interesting
b. **honest**   Fair and upright

No matter how (1) _____ and boring your job is, you should al-

ways put in an (2) _____ day's work.

c. **character**   A person in a book, play, or other work
d. **movie**   A motion picture
e. **stunt**   A feat requiring unusual skill

Alvin has a part in the new (3) _____. He plays a wild

(4) _____ who performs a dangerous (5) _____ in an

airplane.

f. **action**   Activity or quick movement
g. **actor**   A person who performs on the stage, in movies, on televi-
                  sion, or over the radio
h. **cast**   All the actors in a play, movie, or other such work

There was plenty of (6) _____ in that movie on television last

night. I read that one (7) _____ in the (8) _____ was

hurt while performing a difficult scene.

——START THE PLAYER——

Proper Nouns

Mary Wilson	Bill	Sue

_____PREVIEW_____
1. Read the title and look at the picture.
2. Read the first four paragraphs.
3. Then answer questions 9 and 10.
4. When you have finished, start the player.

An Honest Day's Work

by Jane Claypool Miner

Mary Wilson stood with other stunt people who would be working on the movie. When the boss called her name, she ran to him. She wanted to look young.

The boss asked, "How old are you now, Mary? Forty? Forty-five?"

"I'm young enough for this part," Mary answered. "I can ride and jump better than any of the others."

The boss shook his head. "I don't know, Mary. You're good but you're getting too old to be a stunt woman in the movies. Think you can do it?"

Answer questions 9 and 10.

9. Mary ran to the boss when he called her because
   a. she was in a hurry.
   b. she was supposed to run.
   c. somebody was chasing her.
   d. she wanted to look young.

10. The boss
   a. thought Mary would do the best stunt.
   b. was afraid Mary was too old to do the stunt.
   c. didn't like Mary.
   d. had never worked with Mary before.

_____START THE PLAYER_____

_____ COMPREHENSION CHECK _____

Directions: Write or circle the letter of your choice.

11. Mary Wilson had been a stunt woman for
    a. forty years.
    b. forty-five years.
    c. twenty years.
    d. twenty-five years.

12. Bill was
    a. Mary's old boss.
    b. an actor with whom Mary had worked.
    c. a stunt man.
    d. an outlaw.

13. Write or circle the letters of **all** the things that are true about Mary's stunt.
    a. Bill and Mary chase a bank robber.
    b. Bill falls off his horse.
    c. Mary jumps on the outlaw's horse.
    d. Mary fights with the outlaw and knocks her to the ground.
    e. Mary's horse runs away with her.
    f. Mary grabs a tree branch and swings down to the ground.
    g. Mary shoots and kills the outlaw.

14. Bill was afraid that
    a. Mary would mess up his daughter's stunt.
    b. Mary would hurt herself.
    c. Sue would hurt Mary.
    d. he couldn't keep up with Mary.

15. What went wrong with the stunt?
    a. Mary was going too slow.
    b. The horse ran away with Mary.
    c. Sue's timing was off.
    d. Mary fell out of the tree.

16. Write or circle the letters of **all** the things that Mary did to help Sue.
    a. She shouted at Sue to slow down.
    b. She made Sue's horse go slower.
    c. She made her own horse go faster.
    d. She kept Sue from falling off her horse.
    e. She helped Sue fall where she was supposed to fall.

▲17. Mary proved she was a good stunt woman by
    a. doing the stunt exactly the way it had been planned.
    b. helping Sue in such a way that no one knew Sue was in trouble.
    c. making Sue look bad.
    d. doing a stunt nobody had done before.

●18. This story is mainly about
    a. a middle-aged stunt woman who proves that she's still good at her job.
    b. an actor who will do anything to show his love for his daughter.
    c. a boss who won't give a job to a middle-aged stunt woman.
    d. a young stunt woman who tries to show that she is better than a middle-aged stunt woman.

Check your answers with the key.

_____ START THE PLAYER _____

●●●●●●●●

Mary Wilson stood with other stunt people who would be working on the movie. When the boss called her name, she ran to him. She wanted to look young.

The boss asked, "How old are you now, Mary? Forty? Forty-five?"

"I'm young enough for this part," Mary answered. "I can ride and jump better than any of the others."

The boss shook his head. "I don't know, Mary. You're good but you're getting too old to be a stunt woman in the movies. Think you can do it?"

"Sure," Mary answered. "I've been working as a stunt woman for twenty-five years, and I'm used to the action."

"OK," the boss said. "But make it good. There's plenty of action in this movie. If I make any of the stunts easy for you, I'll end up with a dull movie."

"You'll get an honest day's work," Mary said angrily as she stormed away. She took a seat near some of the actors.

One of the actors said, "Hi, Mary. I haven't seen you for a long time. Where have you been?"

"Bill, I'll be honest with you. I wasn't going to do this type of work anymore, but I just couldn't get used to that desk job I had. I need to be out here where the action is. That's my way of staying young."

Bill laughed. "You'll always be young, Mary. You look just like you did the first time we worked together. Do you remember that movie?"

Mary laughed. "That was the one where you played the mean character who set the barn on fire. I had to ride a stallion through that fire to safety."

Bill nodded. "Well, you and I are on the same side of the law in this movie. We'll be chasing an outlaw—a woman who has just held up the bank. You're the one who catches up with her. You jump on her horse,

fight with her, and she falls to the ground. But your horse runs away with you. Not being able to slow the horse down, you grab on to a tree branch and swing down to safety as the horse gallops off." Bill was thoughtful for a moment. Then he said, "Do you think you'll have trouble, Mary?"

Mary's angry eyes flashed at Bill. "I've done bigger stunts than that!"

"Don't get mad, Mary. I guess I'm jumpy because the stunt woman you have to fight is my daughter, Sue."

"Sue?" Mary said. "The last time I saw Sue she was . . ."

"She's twenty years old. This is her first big job."

"And you're afraid I'll mess it up for her," Mary said. "I won't. I promise you."

Bill walked away and Mary became lost in thought. She had to admit that she felt a little out of things. Funny how just a few years ago she'd felt as young as any of them.

But Mary didn't have much time to think about it because the horses were being brought out. Mary climbed onto hers. She felt good again. She felt young. Mary saw Sue climbing onto her horse.

Mary was supposed to jump onto Sue's horse when they passed the church. They would pretend to fight and Sue would fall off into a sand pile. Then Sue's part would be over and Mary would finish her stunt.

Mary grinned at Sue and waved her hand. Sue waved back. Then the cast took their places.

Everything happened very fast after that. She'd been so worried about being old that she forgot Sue was very new. Mary felt great as she rode down the road, but she could see that Sue was in trouble. Her timing was off. She was going much too fast. By the time Mary would catch up with her, Sue would be falling on dirt instead of the sand pile. Mary knew that Sue could get hurt if

Go on to the next page

she fell the wrong way on the hard dirt.

Mary made her horse go faster so that she could catch up with Sue at the right spot. As Mary jumped on Sue's horse, Sue almost fell off. Mary grabbed her and made it look like part of the fight.

Mary held on to Sue as she faked the fight. She held her until they came to the spot where Sue was supposed to fall. Then Mary let her go. Mary was sure it looked OK. The action would be good in the movie.

Mary was going to make sure that the rest of her stunt looked just as good. She rode the horse to make it look like she had no control. When she got to the tree branches, she grabbed on and swung down to the ground.

She heard someone yell, "That's a take!"

Mary smiled to herself. "I gave them their money's worth. They got an honest day's work."

_____**START THE PLAYER**_____

19. Number the events to show the correct sequence.
    a. _____ Mary jumps onto Sue's horse, and Sue almost falls off.
    b. _____ While talking to Bill about the stunt, Mary finds out that Bill is afraid she will mess things up for his daughter, Sue.
    c. _____ Mary finishes her part of the stunt.
    d. _____ As the stunt begins, Mary sees that Sue is going too fast and will fall in the wrong place.
    e. _____ The boss tells Mary he thinks she is too old to be a stunt woman.
    f. _____ During the fight, Mary holds Sue on the horse until they reach the right spot.
    g. _____ Mary makes her horse go faster and catches up with Sue at the right spot.

_____**START THE PLAYER**_____

▲20. What is the problem or conflict?
    a. This is Sue's first big job.
    b. Mary doesn't like her desk job.
    c. People feel Mary is too old to be a stunt woman.
    d. Bill doesn't like playing a mean character.

_____**START THE PLAYER**_____

▲21. What events led to the conflict? (How did the author let you know that people felt Mary was too old to do the stunt?)

_____

_____**START THE PLAYER**_____

▲22. The climax of the story happens when
    a. someone on the film crew yells, "That's a take!"
    b. Mary has to admit that she feels a little out of things.
    c. Sue's timing is off.
    d. Mary must do more than her share to keep the stunt from failing.

_____**START THE PLAYER**_____

▲23. What is the conclusion of the story?
    a. Mary saves the day, thereby proving she's not too old to be a stunt woman.
    b. Sue ruins the stunt but proves she can act well.
    c. Sue's timing is off.
    d. Mary shows that she is too old to be a stunt woman.

_____**START THE PLAYER**_____

PRACTICE

Understanding Plot

Directions: Read the story. Then answer the questions.

Detective Dan Regan was hot on the trail of a thief who had stolen $250,000 worth of diamonds. Regan had a tip that the thief might be hiding out on Oak Beach. Oak Beach was a summer place on the ocean, and nobody lived there in the winter.

When he arrived at Oak Beach, Dan saw smoke coming from one of the little houses by the ocean. He decided to take a closer look. He started to walk across a board over the water. The board broke, and Dan fell into the cold water.

Above him, the door of the house opened and a man came out. "What are you doing here?" he barked.

Dan thought fast and said, "I want to buy a house."

"Not this one," the man said. "Been here for twenty years. I'm not selling!"

Soaking wet, Dan got to his feet.

"You go in and get dry by the stove," the man said. "I'm going to get more wood."

Dan went in and took off his wet pants. Where could he hang them? He found a piece of string and tied it over two nails above the stove. Then he hung up his pants.

The man came back and made some dinner. Dan's pants were dry, and he put them on again and sat down to eat. After the meal, the man washed the dishes while Dan dried them.

When Dan finished, he said, "Where do you want this dish towel?"

The man looked around. "Over there," he said. "On the string over the stove. That's where I always hang it."

Dan quickly pulled his gun. "Reach!" he said.

"What?" screamed the man.

"You haven't lived here for twenty years—not even a week," Dan said. "You never hung a towel on that string before. I put the line up myself only an hour ago!"

1. Number the events to show the correct sequence.
   a. _____ Dan tied a string over the two nails above the stove in order to hang up his pants.
   b. _____ Dan pulled his gun.
   c. _____ Dan went to Oak Beach to catch a thief.
   d. _____ Dan fell into the water, and the man from the house let him in to get dry.
   e. _____ The man told Dan to hang the dish towel on the string over the stove.

▲2. What is the problem or conflict?
   a. Dan Regan wants to buy a house.
   b. Dan Regan falls in the water.
   c. The man from the house is trying to kill Dan Regan.
   d. Dan Regan is trying to catch a thief.

▲3. The climax of the story happens when Dan
   a. discovers that the man is lying.
   b. falls into the water.
   c. hangs his pants up to dry.
   d. eats dinner.

▲4. What is the conclusion of the story?
   a. Dan dries the dishes.
   b. Dan doesn't know where to hang the dish towel.
   c. Dan catches the thief.
   d. The thief gets away.

Check your answers with the key.

____WORD STUDY____

a. **medal**   A piece of metal that is stamped with words or a picture
              and given to someone as an award
b. **remind**   Bring to mind
c. **torn**   Ripped

In a fight last week, Bill's shirt was (1) _____ from his back. He

asked me to (2) _____ him to stay out of fights. If he can do it for

a week, I will give him a (3) _____.

d. **colonel**   A high-ranking army officer
e. **jeep**   A small, sturdy car used by the army
f. **motion**   Act of moving

(4) _____ Atkins ordered his driver to slow down. He explained

that the bouncing (5) _____ of the (6) _____ was

making him feel sick.

g. **eighteen** The number [18] between seventeen and nineteen; eight
              more than ten
h. **position** A planned arrangement of people, especially those fighting
              in the military
i. **rifle**   A long gun
j. **soldier**   Person who serves in the army

The young (7) _____ moved into (8) _____, his

(9) _____ held ready to fire. He thought, "(10) _____

is too young to die."

_____START THE PLAYER_____

Proper Nouns

Captain Logan	Colonel Piedmont

_____PREVIEW_____
1. Read the title and look at the picture.
2. Read the first two paragraphs.
3. Then answer questions 11 and 12.
4. When you have finished, start the player.

At All Costs

by F.X. Duffy, Jr.

"Go!" Logan whispered the command into the evening darkness. Immediately, four soldiers ran across the road, their bodies bent far forward. Logan's heart pounded as he watched their shapes slip through the moonlight. They hit the ground, rolled over, and came up quickly with their rifles ready. They were good men.

As soon as they were in position on the far side of the mountain road, four more soldiers followed with the same expert motions. "Good," Logan thought. "If any of them are nervous, they aren't showing it."

▲11. The soldiers are
a. learning how to fight.
b. practicing shooting their rifles.
c. hiding from the enemy.
d. getting ready for an attack.

▲12. The rest of the story is probably about
a. the men in Logan's command.
b. the attack.
c. how soldiers are trained.
d. a soldier's job.

Answer questions 11 and 12.

_____**START THE PLAYER**_____

____COMPREHENSION CHECK____

Directions: Write or circle the letter of your choice.

13. What is true about the soldiers?
    a. They are not well-prepared.
    b. They'd seen action many times.
    c. They looked nervous.
    d. They are ready to fight.

14. What is true about the plan of attack?
    a. The attack would take place at dawn.
    b. Four soldiers would attack the general's jeep.
    c. The road would be blocked by large rocks.
    d. The fighting would last two days.

15. Logan was
    a. sure the plan would work.
    b. worried that things could go wrong.
    c. afraid his men couldn't do the job.
    d. calm and ready.

16. The last time Logan had seen action
    a. eighteen soldiers in his group had been killed.
    b. he had been wounded.
    c. his shirt had been torn.
    d. he had captured a general.

17. Instead of hiding in a hole, Logan flattened himself against the ground so that he could
    a. see the jeep better.
    b. fire his machine gun.
    c. cover his men from the open.
    d. signal to his men.

▲18. If the general had not been caught in the net, he probably would have
    a. killed himself.
    b. run away.
    c. signaled for help.
    d. fired his machine gun.

▲19. Logan's men threw the jeep over the side of the mountain so that
    a. it would look as if the general had had an accident.
    b. the general couldn't escape in it.
    c. it would explode.
    d. it would not be in their way.

●20. This story is mainly about
    a. World War II.
    b. the attack that won the war.
    c. capturing a general.
    d. being a soldier.

Check your answers with the key.

____START THE PLAYER____

●●●●A●●●●

"Go!" Logan whispered the command into the evening darkness. Immediately, four soldiers ran across the road, their bodies bent far forward. Logan's heart pounded as he watched their shapes slip through the moonlight. They hit the ground, rolled over, and came up quickly with their rifles ready. They were good men.

As soon as they were in position on the far side of the mountain road, four more soldiers followed with the same expert motions. "Good," Logan thought. "If any of them are nervous, they aren't showing it."

Weeks of preparation had gone into this night attack far behind enemy lines. Logan's group of hand-picked soldiers were going into action together for the first time. Their spirits were high. They were trained and they were ready.

The moon slid behind a bank of thick clouds. The night turned even darker. "Just how I like it," thought Logan.

In a short while, a jeep driven by one of the enemy's most important generals would come speeding around the narrow bend to Logan's left. If all went as planned, he would be in Logan's hands seconds later. Logan knew: "If anyone can do the job, my men can."

The plan was simple, if a little strange. As soon as the jeep rounded the turn, four of Logan's men now waiting 100 yards above would push some large rocks down onto the road. The enemy general's jeep would have to stop. Then Logan and two teams of men would jump from their hiding places near the road. Using rope nets, they would corral the general before he could grab his gun. Not a shot would be fired. In two days, Logan and his men would be back home, their prize in hand, the job done.

_____START THE PLAYER_____

21. Which of the following words tell the tone of Section A?
    a. Eager
    b. Instructional
    c. Hopeful
    d. Sad
    e. Frightening
    f. Bold
    g. Amusing
    h. Lighthearted

_____START THE PLAYER_____

DA-14

● ● ● ● B ● ● ● ●

Simple, as plans go. If! If the enemy figured that the general had had an accident, that is. And if the general decided to take his fast, night drive alone, as was his habit. And if he didn't open fire with his machine gun. A simple plan, yes, but many things could go wrong.

Logan glanced up at the dark shapes of the rocks. He wondered how they would bounce. "If they bounce wrong," he thought, "we could all be chopped meat!"

"Try to stay calm," Logan told himself. But his body felt cold. The fear rose up from deep inside him, cutting his breath short and leaving his throat dry. He remembered what Colonel Piedmont had said as Logan and his men pulled out three days before: "You must capture the general alive, Captain Logan, and bring him back across enemy lines at all costs."

Logan sighed. The words "at all costs" had reminded him of the last time he had seen action. Eighteen of his old group had been killed. The medal the army had given him hadn't helped Logan forget their faces. It had hung heavily on his chest. Later he tore it off his shirt. But he still felt its weight pulling at him.

His throat was tight. The air around him seemed to die.

_____START THE PLAYER_____

22. Which of the following words tell the tone of Section B?
    a. Cheerful
    b. Brave
    c. Troubled
    d. Fearful
    e. Eager
    f. Bold
    g. Sad
    h. Impatient

_____START THE PLAYER_____

●●●●C●●●●

But the flare of lights in the distance cut short his thought. Logan's eyes hardened. He whistled twice to his men. Then, in a change of plan, he flattened himself against the ground, instead of hiding in the hole he had dug. He would take his chances with the rockslide; his men might need to be covered from the open. Logan took a deep breath and made sure his machine gun was ready.

He looked around quickly, hoping to catch sight of his men. But it was much too dark. Lights bounced off the cliff far to Logan's left. He could make out the sound of a motor. "Twenty seconds, maybe," he figured. His body was still now and his blood ran strong, as only a soldier's can right before action. "Come on, General," he whispered. "We're going to get you!"

The sound of the motor grew very large. Logan held his breath. He heard rocks sliding and a car screeching to a stop. Then he jumped up into the blinding light of the jeep's headlights as his men threw the nets. He yelled once so that the general would turn toward him. The nets came down; it was done.

Logan ran up to see the general's hand caught in one of the nets. He had reached for his machine gun! But his men's timing had been right on the mark. "Tie him up good and tight, boys. We'll throw his jeep over the side and be gone!"

———————**START THE PLAYER**———————

23. Which of the following words tell the tone of Section C?
    a. Sad
    b. Lighthearted
    c. Instructional
    d. Angry
    e. Bold
    f. Exciting
    g. Worried
    h. Frightening

———————**START THE PLAYER**———————

PRACTICE

Understanding Tone

Directions: Read each story. Then answer the questions by writing or circling the letter(s) of your choice.

"He had some nerve," Dorothy thought as she kicked the can, "leaving us like that. He told me he'd always take care of Momma and me. I hate it when grown-ups lie."

Dorothy kicked the can again and again. Each time she thought of her father.

"Dorothy," Mrs. Maloney said, coming across the street. "We're all so sorry. I guess you'll have to help your Momma now."

"I'm too young to have to take care of anybody. Why did this have to happen to me? Why now?" These were Dorothy's thoughts, but to Mrs. Maloney she said, "I know."

Dorothy tried kicking the can again. Instead, her foot hit the sidewalk. It hurt so much that she began to cry. "It's all your fault, Papa," she cried. "I hate you. No, I love you. I miss you so much. Why'd you have to die?"

1. Which of the following words tell the tone of this story?
   - a. Angry
   - b. Funny
   - c. Sad
   - d. Friendly
   - e. Businesslike
   - f. Lighthearted

Writing a newspaper story isn't difficult if you ask the right questions. They are: what, where, when, who, and why.

First, you must decide **what** the story will be about. For example, you might choose to write about a frog-jumping contest.

Your first question would be: "**Where** is the contest being held?" Is it near town or far away? How do they get the frogs there? Will people have trouble finding the place?

"**When** is the contest?" should come next.

You must find out the day of the month and time of day.

Then you need to ask, "**Who**'s running it?" Find out where they're from and how they became interested in frog-jumping.

Finally, you'll have to ask **why** anyone would want to run, take part in, or watch a frog-jumping contest.

One last pointer: Don't give your opinion. You might think frog jumping is silly, but you shouldn't say so to your readers.

2. Which one of the following tells the tone of this story?
   - a. Angry
   - b. Lighthearted
   - c. Courageous
   - d. Sad
   - e. Instructional
   - f. Fearful

Check your answers with the key.

The Dying Leaves

_____WORD STUDY_____

a. **bushel**   A large amount; specifically, it's a dry measure equal to 32 quarts

b. **October**   The tenth month of the year

In the month of (1) _____, we gathered a (2) _____ of

ripe apples.

c. **responsible**   To have a duty to someone

d. **anger**   The feeling you have when you are angry

e. **drugs**   Dangerous, habit-forming chemical substances that people take for the fake feeling of well-being they give

f. **afford**   To be able to bear the results of

Jane felt much fear and (3) _____ when she learned that her son

was taking (4) _____. She felt (5) _____ for him and

couldn't (6) _____ to lose him.

g. **expensive**   Costing a large amount of money

h. **future**   Time that is yet to come

That eating place is too (7) _____ for us now. We will wait and

eat there in the (8) _____.

_____START THE PLAYER_____

Proper Nouns

Carla	David	Lenny's

The Dying Leaves

by Daniel J. Domoff

A cool October breeze drifted in through the kitchen window. The scents of autumn filled the room—the dry sweetness of dying leaves, the woodsy smoke of evening fires. "Autumn," Carla thought. "The leaves die and scatter along lonely streets."

Answer questions 9 and 10.

9. What does this paragraph tell you about the story?
   a. There are two characters in the story.
   b. The story takes place in autumn.
   c. Someone will die in the story.
   d. Carla's favorite month is October.

▲10. You can tell by looking at the picture that
   a. the two people are married.
   b. the man knows that the woman is there.
   c. the woman is angry at the man.
   d. the woman is surprised by something the man has done.

_____START THE PLAYER_____

●●●●A●●●●

A cool October breeze drifted in through the kitchen window. The scents of autumn filled the room—the dry sweetness of dying leaves, the woodsy smoke of evening fires. "Autumn," Carla thought. "The leaves die and scatter along lonely streets."

"Did you say something?" David's voice broke into Carla's thoughts.

Carla looked up at her brother who stood washing the dishes left over from breakfast. "No," Carla said. "I didn't say anything. Is there anything you want to talk about?"

"No!" David answered almost too quickly.

Then he almost dropped a plate through his wet hands, but he caught it before it fell.

Carla thought, "David seems nervous. Mom's death was too much for him. So soon after Dad's." Carla watched her brother carefully. "Are you nervous, David?"

David looked at Carla once again. "Yes, I guess a little."

———START THE PLAYER———

11. What are the things David did that made Carla think he was nervous? (Write or circle the letters of **all** correct answers.)
   a. He washed the dishes.
   b. He almost dropped a plate.
   c. He was looking at the autumn leaves.
   d. He was too quick to answer "no" when Carla asked if he wanted to talk.
   e. His voice was shaky.

12. What did Carla conclude was making David nervous?
   a. He was afraid of dropping more dishes.
   b. He didn't like to be questioned.
   c. He was upset by the death of their mother, which came so soon after their father's.
   d. He didn't like autumn because of all the dying leaves.

———START THE PLAYER———

"I worry about you," Carla told her brother.

"Well, don't," said David. "I'm 20, remember. You may be my big sister, but you're not responsible for me."

"Okay," said Carla. "Just don't do anything stupid."

"What do you mean?"

Carla couldn't tell him what she was really thinking. And, after all, he had been off of drugs for three years. She must trust him.

"With Mom and Dad both dead, all we've got left is each other. I can't afford to lose my only brother, too."

David smiled. "I'm okay, Sis. Believe me. I miss them both. I cry at night. But I'm okay. There's a whole future for me. For you, too. Don't worry."

David left the kitchen and went to his room. Carla heard the closet open and close, and then a drawer.

Carla walked quietly toward David's room. Standing at the door, she watched David take a small envelope out of his drawer. "David," Carla said.

"What!" David jumped around and in the same move pushed the envelope into his pocket. "Don't come up on me like that, Carla!"

"What's in that envelope?" said Carla.

"Nothing," David shot back. He was angry.

"Are you going out?" Carla asked.

"Yes, I am," said David.

"Where?" she said.

"That's my business," said David.

"By the way, I won't be home for dinner." Then he walked out of the room, up the hall, and out of the house.

Carla gazed about. She thought, "He's nervous. And that envelope . . ." Then her eyes flickered, and, for a moment, burned with understanding. "Drugs! Oh no! Mom and Dad, forgive me. David couldn't hold himself together. He's on drugs again!"

_____START THE PLAYER_____

13. What conclusion did Carla draw about David?
    a. He was on drugs.
    b. He was spending too much money eating out.
    c. He was leaving home for good.
    d. He was going out to mail a letter.

_____START THE PLAYER_____

14. What did Carla know about David that led her to her conclusion?
    a. He had been using drugs on and off for three years.
    b. He had been on drugs three years ago.
    c. His friends were always trying to get David to take drugs.
    d. He always kept drugs in his room.

15. What are the things David did that led Carla to her conclusion? (Write or circle the letters of **all** correct answers.)
    a. He cried every night.
    b. He tried to hide an envelope from her.
    c. He got angry and wouldn't give her a straight answer when she asked him what was in the envelope.
    d. He told her not to worry about him.
    e. He wouldn't tell her where he was going.
    f. He walked out of the house without saying a word to her.

_____START THE PLAYER_____

●●●●C●●●●

All at once, fear, anger, and sadness soared through her. She searched through David's closet and his drawers. She even looked under the bed. She found nothing.

Tired and scared, Carla dropped onto her brother's bed and cried—for her dead parents, for her brother, and for herself. When she finally stopped crying, the autumn evening outside the window had turned to night.

Slowly, like a woman much older than 23, Carla got up. Then remembering that David said he wouldn't be home for dinner, she ran to the door and went out of the house. Seeing the bushels of dead leaves piled in the street made her move more quickly. She had had her fill of death.

Carla raced down to the strip of eating places where she knew she might find David. She went into Lenny's, a fast-food place on Third Street. No David. Then Carla ran to the healthfood place on the corner. Again, no David. "If he's not here and he's not at Lenny's, then he might be at that expensive place he likes on Main."

Carla got there in five minutes. It was a dark place, with quiet, cozy corners where no one could see you. She walked slowly, looking carefully at each table for her brother.

And suddenly, there was David, sitting with someone by a dark wall. Carla, unseen, moved closer. She watched as David passed the tiny envelope to the other person. Carla tried to hear what they were saying. And only then did she see that the person with David was a young woman.

"The ring is beautiful, David," she said.

"I love you," Carla heard her brother say.

"What about your sister?" the young woman asked.

"She'll manage," Carla heard David say. "I'll tell her about you tonight. She still feels bad about Mom and Dad. But she'll be okay."

Still unseen, Carla turned and left. Out on the street, she felt the cool breeze once again. Suddenly, Carla laughed out loud. And then she ran, laughing, back toward home. When she reached her street, she jumped into a pile of dead leaves and rolled in them like a small girl. And then she rose up from the dead leaves. Her heart singing, she looked up to watch the moon riding across the sky like a big, bright promise.

_____START THE PLAYER_____

16. What did Carla see David do?
    a. Pass an envelope of drugs to a friend
    b. Sit in the dark by himself
    c. Give a ring to a young woman
    d. Eat a big dinner

▲17. What do you know about David?
    a. He is still on drugs.
    b. He will never get over his mother's death.
    c. He does not care about Carla.
    d. He loves and wants to marry the young woman.

18. David felt that Carla
    a. would be angry.
    b. would be O.K.
    c. didn't care about him.
    d. was watching him.

▲19. Why was Carla so happy at the end of the story?
    a. She knew that she didn't have to worry about David any longer.
    b. She heard someone singing a song that she liked.
    c. She loved autumn more than any other season.
    d. She was glad to be rid of her brother once and for all.

_____START THE PLAYER_____

▲20. What conclusion can you draw?
    a. Carla will not want David to marry the young woman.
    b. Both Carla and David will get over their parents' deaths.
    c. David will go back on drugs sooner or later.
    d. Both Carla and David will have nervous breakdowns.

_____START THE PLAYER_____

_____COMPREHENSION CHECK_____

Directions: Write or circle the letter of your choice.

21. David hid an envelope
    a. in his drawer.
    b. in the closet.
    c. under the bed.
    d. in his pocket.

▲22. Why couldn't Carla tell David she thought he was on drugs?
    a. He would think she wanted drugs too.
    b. She was too nervous to tell him.
    c. She didn't want him to think she didn't trust him.
    d. He would hit her.

▲23. By looking for David, Carla showed that she
    a. didn't care what happened to him.
    b. wanted to help him.
    c. wanted drugs too.
    d. wanted to go out for dinner.

24. David left the house because he wanted to
    a. get away from Carla.
    b. buy drugs.
    c. give a ring to his girlfriend.
    d. eat dinner out.

25. Where did Carla find David?
    a. At an expensive place on Main Street
    b. At Lenny's
    c. At a healthfood place
    d. At a drug seller's home

26. When will David tell Carla about the girl he loves?
    a. That night
    b. Never
    c. The following week
    d. In a month

▲27. Carla jumped in the leaves because she
    a. was hiding from David.
    b. was happy.
    c. wanted to die with the dying leaves.
    d. wanted to be a small girl again.

●28. This story is mainly about a woman who
    a. helped her brother get off drugs.
    b. took care of her brother after their parents died.
    c. wanted her brother to take care of her after their parents died.
    d. was worried about her brother because she thought he was taking drugs.

Check your answers with the key.

Go on to the next page.

PRACTICE

Drawing Conclusions

Directions: Read the story a section at a time. Then answer the questions by writing or circling the letter(s) of your choice.

Andy Hennessy and John Lipton were two gold miners back in the 1840s. After striking it rich, they were never seen apart—not so much because of friendship, but because each wanted to keep a sharp eye on the other.

They had agreed, you see, that whoever outlived the other would get the dead man's money. By age 95, both were barely hanging on to the thread of life, as each waited for the other to die first.

The day finally arrived when John didn't make it down to breakfast. Andy hurried to John's bedroom. There lay John Lipton, pale as a ghost.

1. What conclusion did Andy reach about John?
   a. John was hungry.
   b. John was about to die.
   c. John wasn't very sick.
   d. John was a good actor.

"You look terrible," Andy said, managing to hide a smile. "Would you like a little breakfast?"

"A boiled egg and a cup of tea," replied John bravely.

But when Andy returned with the egg and tea, John was too weak to eat.

"Listen to me," Andy said worriedly. "Do you remember our arrangement?"

"What arrangement?" whispered John, struggling for air.

"The money," Andy fairly shouted. "Whoever goes first leaves all his money to the other. Tell me quick. Where's the money? Hurry, man, before it's too late!"

▲2. What were **all** the things John did that led Andy to draw this conclusion?
   a. John didn't make it down to breakfast.
   b. He was as pale as a ghost.
   c. He asked for breakfast.
   d. He couldn't eat.
   e. He talked in a whisper and struggled for air.
   f. He didn't hear Andy when Andy asked about the arrangement.

"You first," whispered John. "Where's your money?"

"Under the floorboards in my room," Andy quickly said. "Now—what about you?"

"Sorry, old friend," said John. "I spent every last dime of it."

"Why you mean, blackhearted bag of bones!" Andy screamed. He rose from his chair and danced about in anger, yelling names at John. Suddenly he grabbed at his chest and pitched to the floor. He lay there, as dead as a door nail.

John Lipton leaped out of bed, shouting to all the world: "It worked! It worked! Got that old tightwad at last."

▲3. Why did John tell Andy that he had spent the money?
   a. Because he really had spent it
   b. To make Andy leave him alone
   c. To make Andy get excited with anger
   d. To keep Andy from getting his money after he was dead

▲4. What conclusion can you draw about John Lipton?
   a. He wasn't as mean as Andy Hennessey.
   b. He was skinnier than Andy.
   c. He was a big spender.
   d. He'd planned all along to get rid of Andy.

Check your answers with the key.

DA-16
Recognizing Methods of Persuasion

——WORD STUDY——

a. **credit** — Having to do with buying without paying until later
b. **crew** — Group of people acting together
c. **neighborhood** — The area around where someone lives
d. **tide** — The waters of the ocean

A whole (1) _____ of friends from my (2) _____ de-

cided to stop using (3) _____ cards. We tore the cards up into

little bits and threw them into the (4) _____.

e. **bare** — Plain, simple
f. **shallow** — Not honest, misleading
g. **stern** — Hard and unfeeling

"That was a (5) _____ trick to play on Dan," said Kumi in a

(6) _____ voice. "The (7) _____ fact is Dan believed

what you told him."

h. **ad** — Notice that tries to sell something
i. **product** — Something made or grown
j. **toothpaste** — Paste used in cleaning the teeth

I am so tired of each (8) _____ for (9) _____ shown

on television these days. Each (10) _____ is supposed to be better

than the next, yet they're really all the same.

——START THE PLAYER——

_____PREVIEW_____
1. Read the title and look at the picture.
2. Read the first paragraph.
3. Then answer questions 11 and 12.
4. When you have finished, start the player.

Selling the Truth?

by Cole Gagne

We buy something because we need it. Or do we? Maybe we just think we need it. Every day, on television, in newspapers, in magazines, in signs we see on the street, people try to sell us things. If it is something that we need, then they tell us that the way they make it is better than the way anyone else makes it. If it is something that we don't need, then they try to make us think we do need it. How do they make up our minds for us? They do this in many different ways.

Answer questions 11 and 12.

11. From the preview, you know this story is going to tell you
    a. why people try to sell you products you don't need.
    b. how certain products are better than others.
    c. how ads make you want to buy products.
    d. why you should watch the ads on television.

12. Write the missing words.
    If the product is something you (a) _____, the ads tell you they make it (b) _____ than anyone else. If it is something you don't need, the ads make you (c) _____ you do need it.

_____START THE PLAYER_____

COMPREHENSION CHECK

Directions: Write or circle the letter of your choice.

13. Why do some car ads show a car in front of a high-class, expensive house with rich people wearing expensive clothes?
    a. To give you the idea that the car is very expensive
    b. To give you the idea that the car is high-class
    c. To give you the idea that you can't own the car unless you are rich
    d. To give you the idea that the car is very well made

▲14. If a famous person tries to sell you something, you would probably
    a. listen to what that person has to say.
    b. not buy the product.
    c. not listen at all.
    d. think that person doesn't know about the product.

▲15. The companies who sell canned or frozen foods want the working mother to use their products because
    a. they know their foods taste better than fresh foods.
    b. they are really in business to help the working mother.
    c. they know their foods are healthier than fresh foods.
    d. that's how they make money.

▲16. The author thinks that most of the breakfast foods in ads meant for children
    a. are very healthful.
    b. are not healthful at all.
    c. do not taste good.
    d. taste delicious.

17. Ads for soft drinks usually show people
    a. having fun.
    b. eating dinner.
    c. driving a car.
    d. sitting quietly at home.

18. Most toothpaste ads tell you
    a. to use their toothpaste to be special.
    b. their product will give you a great smile.
    c. anything except why their product helps clean teeth better than any other toothpaste.
    d. the best way to use their product.

19. When you read or watch an ad, you should
    a. go right out and buy the product.
    b. try the product to see if you like it.
    c. look to see if the company is playing a trick on you.
    d. get all the facts before you buy the product.

▲20. From this story, you know that many ads
    a. play tricks on you.
    b. tell you all the facts.
    c. make you think twice before buying a product.
    d. show people having fun.

●21. This story is mainly about how
    a. to sell a product.
    b. to buy a product.
    c. ads push you to buy a product.
    d. to listen to ads.

Check your answers with the key.

START THE PLAYER

Everybody's Doing It

Snob Appeal

Famous or Professional People

Good Feelings

Fear

●●●●A●●●●

We buy something because we need it. Or do we? Maybe we just think we need it. Every day, on television, in newspapers, in magazines, in signs we see on the street, people try to sell us things. If it is something that we need, then they tell us that the way they make it is better than the way anyone else makes it. If it is something that we don't need, then they try to make us think we do need it. How do they make up our minds for us? They do this in many different ways.

Take cars, for example. We might see a car sitting on a lawn in front of a huge, high-class home. The people standing around the car are very well-dressed. In fact, everything around the car looks very expensive. The people selling the car hope that we'll get the idea that the car is high-class too. We'd never get this idea if we saw the car waiting in line for gas or if we saw the driver fixing a flat tire. We do those things all the time if we own a car. But that car wouldn't seem quite as high-class in those settings, would it?

_____START THE PLAYER_____

22. What method of persuasion is used in this section?
    a. Everybody's Doing It
    b. Snob Appeal
    c. Famous or Professional People
    d. Good Feelings
    e. Fear

_____START THE PLAYER_____

●●●●B●●●●

We can't turn on the television without seeing someone trying to sell us food. That someone might be a famous actor. He tells us how great the food is and that he always eats it. What does an actor know about food? Probably no more than we do. But a famous face will sell a product. After all, people think if it's good enough for him, then it's good enough for us.

23. What method of persuasion is used in this section?
    a. Everybody's Doing It
    b. Snob Appeal
    c. Famous or Professional People
    d. Good Feelings
    e. Fear

_____START THE PLAYER_____

●●●●C●●●●

More and more women are working today. They are enjoying their new-found freedom and power. So when food is sold on television, we see the working mother coming home and just opening a can or heating something from the freezer. They want women to think, "If it's all right for that working woman to use frozen foods, then it's all right for me." How good is that food for you? No one says anything about that. Does it even taste good? Everyone on television enjoys it. But everyone on television is being paid to eat it.

24. What method of persuasion is used in this section?
    a. Everybody's Doing It
    b. Snob Appeal
    c. Famous or Professional People
    d. Good Feelings
    e. Fear

●●●●D●●●●

Children are very easily taken in by television ads for food. They are told that every kid on the block eats a certain breakfast food. If everybody is eating that food, they don't want to be left out.

They see children eat the breakfast food and then run out and play around the neighborhood all day. What the ads don't say is that if the children ate only that food, they'd be too weak to walk out the door. That's why it's now a law to show toast, milk, and juice being eaten with that breakfast food.

25. What method of persuasion is used in this section?
    a. Everybody's Doing It
    b. Snob Appeal
    c. Famous or Professional People
    d. Good Feelings
    e. Fear

●●●●E●●●●

And what about all those happy kids having fun at the beach? We see the whole crew downing soft drinks as they leap into the tide. All the fun things they do have nothing to do with drinking that stuff. But we keep seeing those two pictures together: fun at the beach and soft drinks. If we see that enough, then when we go to the beach, we start thinking that we're not really having fun if we're without that soft drink.

26. What method of persuasion is used in this section?
    a. Everybody's Doing It
    b. Snob Appeal
    c. Famous or Professional People
    d. Good Feelings
    e. Fear

_____START THE PLAYER_____

••••F••••

Does this television ad sound familiar? A man or woman has no luck getting a date with the person he or she really wants. A friend says, "Brush your teeth with this!" He or she uses it and the next day is having a great time dating that special person. But we're never told what it is about that toothpaste that helps it clean teeth better than any other toothpaste. Could it be because nothing about it is special? Rather than admit that, the people who sell the toothpaste show it doing all kinds of things that have nothing to do with the good health of your teeth.

27. What method of persuasion is used in this section?
    a. Everybody's Doing It
    b. Snob Appeal
    c. Famous or Professional People
    d. Good Feelings
    e. Fear

••••G••••

Sometimes ads will warn us that something terrible will happen to us if we don't use a particular product. For example, a woman doesn't have her credit card with her when she leaves her house. Her car gets stuck and is taken to a garage. It will cost $200 to fix the car and the woman has nowhere near that amount of money on her. A stern voice comes on and says, "Next time, Mary will remember to take her credit card with her. How about you?" If the ad doesn't frighten us, then the voice does.

When we see or listen to an ad we should ask ourselves, "What is the truth?" We mustn't fall for shallow tricks. Instead, we must make sure that we get the bare facts about the product. If the ad doesn't give these facts, we'd better think twice before we buy the product.

28. What method of persuasion is used in this section?
    a. Everybody's Doing It
    b. Snob Appeal
    c. Famous or Professional People
    d. Good Feelings
    e. Fear

———START THE PLAYER———

PRACTICE

Recognizing Methods of Persuasion

Directions: Read each section. Then answer each question by writing or circling the letter of your choice.

"Ms. Fisher, I have a great idea for selling your Gold Medal Sparkling Water," the ad-man said.

"Well, let's hear it."

"The ad shows a well-to-do woman and her guests sitting around her private pool in back of her huge home. Everyone is drinking Gold Medal. Then she looks toward the camera and says, 'I serve only the best at my parties.'"

1. What method of persuasion is used in this section?
   a. Everybody's Doing It
   b. Snob Appeal
   c. Famous or Professional People
   d. Good Feelings
   e. Fear

"Let just one of those people in, and it will be the end of the neighborhood. You'll see. They start to come in slowly, and before you know it, they've taken over." Mr. Adams was speaking to a meeting at Town Hall. "Do you want your children playing with theirs? Do you want your house to be worth less? Do you want more robberies to take place around here? Of course, you don't. That's why we must stop them now."

2. What method of persuasion is used in this section?
   a. Everybody's Doing It
   b. Snob Appeal
   c. Famous or Professional People
   d. Good Feelings
   e. Fear

"Mr. Ramirez," Maria was saying, "all the storekeepers on the block use my newspaper to tell the people of this town about their stores. You should too."

3. What method of persuasion is used in this section?
   a. Everybody's Doing It
   b. Snob Appeal
   c. Famous or Professional People
   d. Good Feelings
   e. Fear

"I meant to ask you," Loretta said to Art, "what made you decide that you wanted Ronald Russel for President?"

"That's simple," Art answered. "Wayne Holt, the greatest country singer around, said that he liked Ronald Russel. I decided that if he was good enough for Wayne Holt, he was good enough for me."

4. What method of persuasion is used in this section?
   a. Everybody's Doing It
   b. Snob Appeal
   c. Famous or Professional People
   d. Good Feelings
   e. Fear

"Jack," Susan called, "don't forget to pick up the Dr. Crown soda on your way home."

"Why Dr. Crown?"

"Well, I guess it was that ad on T.V. You know, the one with all those young people at the circus. They were drinking Dr. Crown and having a wonderful time. I thought we should try Dr. Crown for Joey's birthday party."

5. What method of persuasion is used in this section?
   a. Everybody's Doing It
   b. Snob Appeal
   c. Famous or Professional People
   d. Good Feelings
   e. Fear

Check your answers with the key.

DA-17

Understanding Author's Message

Rain, Rain . . . Go Away?

_____WORD STUDY_____

a.	**adapt**	Adjust to special conditions
b.	**blizzard**	A snowstorm with strong, cold winds
c.	**icy**	Very cold and covered with ice
d.	**temperature**	How hot or cold something is

During the (1)_____ , the people of Jackson complained

about the freezing cold (2)_____ and (3)_____

road conditions. But in a few days, the townspeople were able to

(4) _____well.

e.	**Eskimo**	A member of a group of people who live in the Arctic regions of North America and northeastern Asia;*Inuit* is now the preferred term to refer to these people.
f.	**northern**	Of the north
g.	**polar**	Having to do with the North or South Pole
h.	**zone**	A particular area of the earth

I had never met an (5)_____ before my trip to Alaska, which

is the most (6)_____ state of the United States. Because

it is close to the North Pole, Alaska is in an area known as the

(7)_____ (8)_____ .

_____ **START THE PLAYER** _____

Proper Nouns

Death Valley	Hopi	New Jersey
California	Arizona	San Francisco

112

_____PREVIEW_____
1. Read the title and look at the picture.
2. Read the first two paragraphs.
3. Then answer questions 9 and 10.
4. When you have finished, start the player.

Rain, Rain . . . Go Away?

by Sylvia P. Bloch

Somewhere a woman wakes up to the sound of rain falling outside. On the radio she hears the announcer giving the day's weather: "It's going to rain all day today, folks. Leave yourselves some extra time for going to work. Large puddles and heavy rains are slowing down traffic. And the weekend? It doesn't look good. The rain should last until Monday."

She groans and turns over. Why bother getting out of bed? Going to work won't be any fun, and the camping trip for this weekend will be off. What was that song she used to sing as a kid—"Rain, rain, go away. Come again some other day." That's right! Who needs this rain, anyway?

Answer questions 9 and 10.

9. The woman is not happy with the rain because
   a. it doesn't look good outdoors when it rains.
   b. she did not leave extra time to get to work.
   c. the sound of the rain has woken her up.
   d. she had planned a camping trip for the weekend.

▲10. This part of the story probably takes place on
   a. Monday.
   b. Thursday.
   c. Friday.
   d. Sunday.

_____START THE PLAYER_____

_____COMPREHENSION CHECK_____

Directions: Write or circle the letter of your choice.

11. The farmer's crops are short, brown, and sickly because
    a. the earth is a wet, dark brown.
    b. there is not enough rain.
    c. the earth is not good enough.
    d. he ran out of supplies.

12. What may depend on the amount of rainfall an area receives?
    a. How many blizzards the area has
    b. The temperature of that area
    c. The types of life forms found in that area
    d. The number of fish in the waters of that area

▲13. Why would it be easier to live in the northern polar region than in a desert?
    a. There is less rainfall in the northern polar region.
    b. It is too difficult to find food in a desert.
    c. Blizzards don't add up to much rainfall.
    d. It's more comfortable in the cold than in the heat.

14. Some desert plants and animals are able to
    a. store water.
    b. live without any water.
    c. make their own water.
    d. do all of the above.

15. In ancient times, people believed they could make rain by
    a. performing magic.
    b. using dry ice.
    c. cooling the air.
    d. leaving it to nature.

16. At the present time, scientists
    a. do a special dance to make rain.
    b. have given up trying to make rain.
    c. can make rain better than nature can.
    d. try to make rain by cooling the air.

17. What are the things that can be done to save water during a dry period? (Write or circle the letters of **all** correct choices.)
    a. Don't bathe.
    b. Fine people who use too much water.
    c. Don't hose down sidewalks.
    d. Don't cook with water.
    e. Don't refill swimming pools.
    f. Don't wash cars.
    g. Save your bath and dish water.
    h. Don't wash dishes.

18. During dry periods in San Francisco and in northern New Jersey,
    a. people moved to other cities.
    b. people paid no attention to water-saving rules.
    c. rules were set up to help save water.
    d. prizes were given to people who saved the most water.

Check your answers with the key.

_____START THE PLAYER_____

▲ 19. The author wrote "Rain, Rain ... Go Away?" in order to
   a. inform.
   b. entertain.
   c. persuade.

────────START THE PLAYER────────

••••A••••

Somewhere a woman wakes up to the sound of rain falling outside. On the radio she hears the announcer giving the day's weather: "It's going to rain all day today, folks. Leave yourselves some extra time for going to work. Large puddles and heavy rains are slowing down traffic. And the weekend? It doesn't look good. The rain should last until Monday."

She groans and turns over. Why bother getting out of bed? Going to work won't be any fun, and the camping trip for this weekend will be off. What was that song she used to sing as a kid—"Rain, rain, go away. Come again some other day." That's right! Who needs this rain, anyway?

But what if the rain goes away and "some other day" doesn't come for a long time? Instead of the scene above, picture this scene in another part of the country.

A farmer leans on his fence, staring out over his fields. Instead of tall, green, healthy plants, he sees short, brown, sickly plants. The earth is not a wet, dark brown—it's dried out, and deep cracks run through it. The farmer turns up his radio and hears: "It will be another hot, sunny day. Still no rain in sight."

He sighs and gloomily wonders what will happen to him and his family this year. With no crops to harvest, where will they get any money? And he might not be able to buy supplies for next year's crops. He wishes it would rain ... for a whole week.

────────START THE PLAYER────────

20. What main point is the author making?
   a. Rain can spoil people's plans.
   b. A farmer depends upon rain to live.
   c. Plants must have rain in order to grow.
   d. Many people don't realize how important rain is.

••••● B ●••••

Just how important is rain? Well, rainfall is so important that in many ways the amount of rainfall controls the way people live. In fact, the types of life forms found in a certain area may depend on the amount of rainfall the area receives.

Two very different areas that receive little rain are the northern polar zone of the earth and the earth's desert areas. It might surprise you to know that part of the cold, icy, northern polar zone gets as little rainfall as one of the hottest, driest areas—Death Valley in California.

In these places where there is little rainfall, life may be very different from the way you know it. The land of Eskimos (Inuit), blizzards, and cold temperatures stays icy for many months of the year. Blizzards don't add up to much rainfall because ten inches of snow is equal to only about one inch of rain. Since this northern land can't be farmed, the Inuit live mainly by hunting and fishing.

In the hot desert, you would find little game to hunt and no waters in which to fish. Only some plants can live in that hot, dry area. Those that do, have very long roots to get the water which lies deep under the ground. Other plants adapt by storing water in their stems and leaves. Likewise, the only animals that can live in the desert are ones that need little water or can store water.

For example, animals such as camels can travel from place to place in the desert because they can store water for a long time.

21. What main point is the author making?
    a. The Inuit live mainly by hunting and fishing.
    b. Only animals and plants that can store water are able to live in the desert.
    c. Rainfall not only controls the way people live in different areas, but it also controls the type of life forms found there.
    d. The northern polar zone and the desert are alike because they get little rain.

_____ START THE PLAYER _____

••••● C ●••••

Can we make rain? In ancient times, people believed in rain magic. They would wear special costumes and paint their bodies. They would send up smoke clouds and use rattles and drums to make the sounds of a rainstorm. The Hopi tribe in Arizona still do a special snake dance every August in order to bring rain and a good harvest.

Today, many experiments are done to try to cool the air so that rain can form. Airplanes unload small drops of a very cold gas that is frozen to a temperature of 109°F below zero (-78.5°C). This gas is often called dry ice. Scientists hope that these icy drops will lower the temperature enough to make rain. But it is difficult to tell if these experiments succeed or not. If it does rain, it might be because it was going to rain to begin with. It is hard to tell who is making the rain, nature or the scientist.

22. What main point is the author making?
    a. Some people do special dances to make rain.
    b. Dry ice is used to cool the air so that rain can form.
    c. People are always looking for ways to make rain.
    d. People still cannot make rain.

_____ START THE PLAYER _____

••• D •••

If we can't develop a way to make rain, what can we do during long dry periods? Years ago, after a long time of very little rain, the city of San Francisco, California, had to come up with ways to save its water. The city government made rules as to how much water each family could use. If people used too much water, they first got a warning, then a fine. It was against the law to hose sidewalks or refill swimming pools. People didn't wash their cars or water the grass. When they took baths and washed dishes, they saved the water. Many of these same rules were used to help save low water supplies in northern New Jersey years later.

Had the woman at the beginning of this story lived in San Francisco or in New Jersey when water supplies were low, she might be singing a very different song from "Rain, rain, go away."

23. What main point is the author making?
   a. People can get fined for using too much water during dry periods.
   b. People must find ways to save water during dry periods.
   c. It is against the law to use water for certain things.
   d. People must save their bath and dish water to use over again.

_____ **START THE PLAYER** _____

▲ 24. What is the author's message?
   a. Some people like rain while others do not.
   b. The amount of rainfall controls the way people live.
   c. We don't have to worry about rain because we can make it any time we want.
   d. Rain is very important, and people shouldn't take it for granted.

_____ **START THE PLAYER** _____

___PRACTICE___
Understanding Author's Message

Directions: Read each part of the story. Then answer the questions by writing or circling the letter of your choice.

Few riders have been more regularly parted from their horses than the Duke of Alburquerque. The Duke liked to race in the Grand National, a race over fences in Liverpool, England. Dividing his time equally between the saddle and the stretcher, this Spanish Duke entered the Grand National seven times with much the same awkward ending. The Duke would start with the others, gallop a short distance, and then wake up in the Liverpool hospital.

In 1952, the Duke fell at the sixth fence and almost broke his neck. In 1963, it was the fourth fence that did him in. Then in the 1965 Grand National, both the Duke and his horse fell. And in 1973, his saddle fell apart. The Duke hung on bravely for eight fences before—as was his habit—going into orbit. People began to think that he'd have a better chance of finishing the race if he went on foot.

1. What main point is the author making?
   a. The Grand National is a race over fences in Liverpool.
   b. The sixth fence is the most dangerous fence in the Grand National.
   c. In the 1973 Grand National, the Duke's saddle fell apart.
   d. The Duke was famous for falling off his horse before the end of the Grand National.

In 1974, having fallen off while training, the Duke surprised the nurses and doctors at the Liverpool hospital by showing up days before he was expected. Not a man to give up, the Duke rode with both a broken leg and collar bone. The Duke later said: "I sat like a bag of potatoes and gave the horse no help." This may explain how he came to finally finish the course. Needless to say, he did not win.

2. What main point is the author making?
   a. The Duke doesn't have enough sense to know when not to race.
   b. Never go to the hospital without making an appointment first.
   c. The Duke sat like a bag of potatoes and gave the horse no help.
   d. The Duke would have won if he hadn't broken his leg.

▲ 3. What is the author's message?
   a. Practice makes perfect.
   b. Riding horses can be dangerous.
   c. Some people never know when to give up.
   d. Everybody loves a winner.

▲ 4. The author wrote this story in order to
   a. inform.
   b. entertain.
   c. persuade.

Check your answers with the key.

It's a Jungle out There

_____WORD STUDY_____

a. **anger**   Strong displeasure or wrath
b. **battle**   Combat or war
c. **warrior**   A person experienced in fighting battles

After the attack on his village, the (1) _____ felt the

(2) _____ within him grow. Now he was ready to go to

(3) _____ with the enemy.

d. **respond**   React
e. **jungle**   A place in which it is difficult to survive
f. **decision**   A making up of one's mind
g. **stress**   Tension, pressure, or strain

The place where I work is a (4) _____ . Because people are

always under (5) _____ , they often (6) _____ to

each other in less than friendly ways. I have made a (7) _____

to leave as soon as I can find a new job.

h. **friendship**   The state of being friends
i. **dignity**   Quality of being worthy
j. **companion**   A comrade or associate

Your (8) _____ means a lot to me. There is no better

(9) _____ than you. When others attack me, you help me keep

my sense of (10) _____ .

_____ START THE PLAYER _____

Proper Nouns

Gloria	George	Ms. Jackson
Mr. Sanchez	Diane	

It's a Jungle out There
by Estelle Kleinman

Have you ever heard someone say, "It's a jungle out there"? If this saying reminds you of the place where you work, you're not alone. Maybe you believe that someone is after your job. Or perhaps you are given so much work to do that you can't possibly get all of it done in time. Or you might think the person you're working for is out to get you. How do you act when such things happen? Actually, there are three ways a person might respond in such cases: they can fight, run, or freeze.

Answer questions 11 and 12.

▲ 11. This story will probably be about
   a. how people respond to stressful things that happen at work.
   b. what it is like to live in the jungle.
   c. different old sayings that might help you in life.
   d. what people can do to find a better job.

12. Which is **not** one of the ways the story says that a person might respond to stress on the job?
   a. Fight
   b. Run
   c. Perform
   d. Freeze

_____ START THE PLAYER _____

COMPREHENSION CHECK

Directions: Write or circle the letter of your choice.

13. Why does Gloria believe that Mr. Sanchez doesn't like her?
    a. He never smiles at her or tells her that she is doing a good job.
    b. Another worker told Gloria that Mr. Sanchez doesn't like her.
    c. He complained to the president of the company about her.
    d. He told her to look for another job.

14. Which happened last?
    a. Gloria thought it a good idea to start recording Mr. Sanchez's every move in writing.
    b. When it was time for Gloria to take her vacation, Mr. Sanchez said she couldn't go.
    c. Mr. Sanchez gave Gloria only a small raise and wrote that she "needs improvement."
    d. Gloria went to the president of the company to complain about Mr. Sanchez.

15. When she felt herself ready to explode, Gloria should have
    a. had it out with Mr. Sanchez once and for all.
    b. thought about all the bad things Mr. Sanchez did to her.
    c. left her job for good.
    d. done something to cool off.

▲16. Why did George turn down the new job?
    a. The pay wasn't very good.
    b. He would have had to work nights.
    c. He was afraid that it would be too difficult for him.
    d. He didn't want to leave his friends.

17. Some experts suggest that a person like George should
    a. make a decision and stick to it.
    b. always do what is easiest.
    c. not be afraid to change his or her mind after making a decision.
    d. not change jobs.

18. Ms. Jackson never chooses Diane to chair a meeting because
    a. Diane freezes when she has to speak in front of a group.
    b. she doesn't like Diane.
    c. Diane is never well prepared.
    d. she wants Diane to work behind the scenes.

▲19. From what you've read, which of the following would probably help Diane?
    a. Having Ms. Jackson help her decide what to say at meetings
    b. Having a friend stand by her when she talks
    c. Telling herself that she knows the material and can talk about it to anyone
    d. Finding a job where she doesn't have to talk in front of groups

● 20. This story is mainly about
    a. people who let their fears stop them from getting ahead at work.
    b. why people are not happy with their jobs.
    c. how people can learn better ways to respond to difficulties at work.
    d. how to avoid fights at work.

Check your answers with the key.

_____ **START THE PLAYER** _____

●●●●● **A** ●●●●●

Have you ever heard someone say, "It's a jungle out there"? If this saying reminds you of the place where you work, you're not alone. Maybe you believe that someone is after your job. Or perhaps you are given so much work to do that you can't possibly get all of it done in time. Or you might think the person you're working for is out to get you. How do you act when such things happen? Actually, there are three ways a person might respond in such cases: they can fight, run, or freeze.

Gloria is a fighter. <u>She believes that the man she works for, Mr. Sanchez, doesn't like her.</u> <u>He never smiles at her or tells her that she is doing a good job.</u> When Mr. Sanchez gave Gloria only a small raise and wrote that she "needs improvement," Gloria was like a warrior ready to do battle. <u>She felt that her dignity was under attack.</u> <u>Wasting no time, Gloria went to the president of the company to complain about Mr. Sanchez.</u> <u>She also thought it a good idea to start recording his every move in writing.</u>

What happened? Mr. Sanchez's anger against Gloria grew, and he got back at her whenever he could. <u>For example, when it was time for her to take her vacation, he told her that she couldn't go because he needed her to work that week.</u> Now, thinking about all the things he has done to her, Gloria just gets more and more upset.

What could Gloria have done to control her anger? She could have asked herself, "What do I win if I fight this person, and what might I lose?" If she did this, she might have realized that fighting with Mr. Sanchez couldn't possibly do her any good. When she felt herself ready to explode, she should have done something to cool off, like going on a break or talking things over with a friend. A good friendship can help get you through many difficult times. Then, after Gloria cooled down, she could have talked to Mr. Sanchez calmly about what was bothering her, and might even have asked him to suggest ways in which she could improve her work.

_____ **START THE PLAYER** _____

21. Write *fact* or *opinion* for each sentence.

a. _____ She believes that the man she works for, Mr. Sanchez, doesn't like her.

b. _____ He never smiles at her or tells her that she is doing a good job.

c. _____ She felt that her dignity was under attack.

d. _____ Wasting no time, Gloria went to the president of the company to complain about Mr. Sanchez.

e. _____ She also thought it a good idea to start recording his every move in writing.

f. _____ For example, when it was time for her to take her vacation, he told her that she couldn't go because he needed her to work that week.

_____ **START THE PLAYER** _____

•••• B ••••

George is a person who runs from anything that might prove difficult. Being bright, he could get a better job, but he is afraid. "I'll probably fail if I try something new," he thinks. He did once find a better-paying job in the company, but turned it down a few days before it was supposed to start. "I think it's for the best," he told a companion. "Who needs the stress?" But that night he couldn't sleep, thinking about the job he lost.

What should people like George do? The first thing he should do is decide if he really wants a better job. If the answer is yes, then he must learn to take on things that are difficult. Some experts feel that the best way to do this is to make a decision and then stick to it. Go ahead and take the new job once you've made up your mind that it's what you really want. Instead of always looking for the easy way, don't be afraid to take the hard way if it's right for you.

22. Write *fact* or *opinion* for each sentence.

a. _____ "I'll probably fail if I try somthing new," he thinks.

b. _____ He did once find a better-paying job in the company, but turned it down a few days before it was supposed to start.

c. _____ "I think it's for the best," he told a companion.

d. _____ But that night he couldn't sleep, thinking about the job he lost.

e. _____ Some experts feel that the best way to do this is to make a decision and then stick to it.

_____ **START THE PLAYER** _____

•••• C ••••

Diane's fear causes her to freeze when she has to speak in front of a group of people. Believing that they will think less of her if she makes mistakes, she can't think of what to say. Knowing Diane's fear, the person she reports to, Ms. Jackson, never chooses Diane to chair a meeting. Though Ms. Jackson gives her work to do behind the scenes, she feels that Diane isn't pulling her weight. Ms. Jackson has talked to Diane about this more than once. Diane knows that she will never go far in the company unless she gets over her fear.

What should Diane do? First, she should ask herself if she's really happy with her job as it is or if she wants to get ahead. If she wants to get ahead, then she must get over her fear. Some experts think that if you're afraid of something, you should force yourself to face it. The more you practice, the easier it will become. Others feel that you must also learn how to calm yourself down before you face something you fear. For example, Diane might want to take a few minutes before speaking to imagine a calm scene or do some deep breathing. Experts also suggest that you stop telling yourself you can't do something; instead, think of what you *can* do.

Go on to the next page. 123

So what do you do when you're upset, afraid, or stressed out at work? Ask yourself, "What do I want to happen?" Then choose the actions that will make this happen. All you have to do is stop and think. If you do that, then you can be in control rather than have your feelings control you. That's the smart thing to do, and you have to be smart to make it in the jungle.

23. Write *fact* or *opinion* for each sentence.

a. _____ Diane's fear causes her to freeze when she has to speak in front of a group of people.

b. _____ Knowing Diane's fear, the person she reports to, Ms. Jackson, never chooses Diane to chair a meeting.

c. _____ Ms. Jackson has talked to Diane about this more than once.

d. _____ Some experts think that if you are afraid of something, you should force yourself to face it.

e. _____ Others feel that you must also learn how to calm yourself down before you face something you fear.

_____ **START THE PLAYER** _____

24. Write *fact* or *opinion* for the underlined part of each sentence.

a. _____ Believing that they will think less of her if she makes mistakes, she can't think of what to say.

b. _____ Though Ms. Jackson gives her work to do behind the scenes, she feels that Diane isn't pulling her weight.

_____ **START THE PLAYER** _____

_____PRACTICE_____

Recognizing Fact and Opinion

Directions: Read the story. Decide which of the underlined parts are fact and which are opinion. Then write the word *fact* or *opinion* for each example in the exercise that follows.

John Van Doren, a banker and playboy, met a famous dancer. He thought she was the most beautiful, most perfect woman in all the world. For many months Van Doren took her to the best places in town. Before long, he was madly in love and wanted to marry her.

But his friends, thinking Van Doren was making a mistake, warned him to be careful. Some of his friends thought that the woman might be after his money. Others felt that, being a dancer, she might be hiding some terrible secret from her past.

Van Doren listened to what all his friends had to say. Not wanting to make a mistake he would later feel sorry about, Van Doren hired a detective to check up on the dancer.

Believing that people would laugh if they knew he had gone to such lengths, Van Doren did not give the detective his real name.

After a few weeks, the detective sent Van Doren the following report:

"The lady in question has a spotless history. Her friends—both off and on the stage—have never been in trouble. Everyone believes them to be honest characters. The only spot on the lady's record is that for the last few months, she has often been seen in the company of a certain banker with a dreadful past. This banker has broken the hearts and disgraced the names of many good women."

Write fact or *opinion* for each sentence or the underlined part of the sentence.

1. _____ John Van Doren, a banker and playboy, met a famous dancer.

2. _____ He thought she was the most beautiful, most perfect woman in all the world.

3. _____ But his friends, thinking Van Doren was making a mistake, warned him to be careful.

4. _____ Others felt that, being a dancer, she might be hiding some terrible secret from her past.

5. _____ Believing that people would laugh if they knew he had gone to such lengths, Van Doren did not give the detective his real name.

6. _____ Everyone believes them to be honest characters.

7. _____ "The only spot on the lady's record is that for the last few months, she has often been seen in the company of a certain banker with a dreadful past."

Check your answers with the key.

Understanding Sensory Images

Snow Luck

———WORD STUDY———

a. **disturb**   Break in upon with noise
b. **grumble**   Make a low, rumbling noise as if annoyed

Angelo began to (1) _____ as he reached to answer the telephone.

He did not like anyone to (2) _____ him while he was working.

c. **flutter**   Move with quick, wavering motions
d. **swoop**   Make a sudden attack
e. **squawk**   Complain loudly

I sat there enjoying the breeze and watching the leaves (3) _____

to the ground. I did not hear my husband (4) _____ down on me

until he started to (5) _____ about my not helping him with the

dinner.

f. **mutter**   Complain or grumble
g. **detour**   A route used when the main road cannot be traveled; anything that has to do with such a route
h. **ski**   Glide over snow by means of narrow strips of wood; one of a pair of such strips of wood
i. **thermos**   A special container that keeps its contents either hot or cold

Coming back from his (6) _____ trip, Joe saw a

(7) _____ sign in the middle of the road ahead. "The main road

would have to be closed just when I wanted to get home early," he began to

(8) _____ to himself. "I'm getting so cold, too. I wish I had a

(9) _____ of nice, hot soup."

———START THE PLAYER———

Proper Nouns

| Joan | Marty | Mountain Top Hotel |

PREVIEW
1. Read the title and look at the picture.
2. Read the first two paragraphs.
3. Then answer questions 10 and 11.
4. When you have finished, start the player.

Snow Luck

by Emilie Lion

The sky was gray and the dark clouds were heavy with the promise of snow. The sharp, biting winter wind swooped down on the dead leaves and sent them fluttering through the air. As the first white, feathery snowflakes began to fall, a small car drove around the bend in the lonely country road and pulled over to the side.

"You did it again, Joan," Marty shouted angrily at the young woman sitting next to him. "You got us lost again. Can't you read and follow a simple map?"

Answer questions 10 and 11.

10. Where are Joan and Marty?
    a. On the wrong side of the road
    b. Near a farmhouse
    c. In the woods
    d. On a lonely country road

▲11. You can tell by the picture that Joan and Marty like to
    a. ice skate.
    b. walk in the country.
    c. ski.
    d. go camping.

_____**START THE PLAYER**_____

_____COMPREHENSION CHECK_____

Directions: Write or circle the letter of your choice.

12. Why did Marty stop the car at the side of the road?
    a. There was too much snow.
    b. He wanted to stop for a thermos of hot soup.
    c. He was lost.
    d. The car wasn't working.

13. Why didn't Marty and Joan drive back to the DETOUR sign?
    a. Joan couldn't read the map.
    b. The car wouldn't start.
    c. It was snowing too hard.
    d. They decided to ski instead.

14. At first, Marty was angry at Joan because
    a. he blamed her for getting them lost.
    b. he didn't want to go on the ski trip.
    c. he didn't like being wrong.
    d. she went past the DETOUR sign.

▲15. Joan was nervous because
    a. Marty was shouting at her.
    b. she was in a hurry to go skiing.
    c. she didn't know where the DE-TOUR sign was.
    d. she knew something was seriously wrong with the car.

16. Why did Joan and Marty put on their skis?
    a. They thought they would find another place to ski.
    b. It was a good day to go skiing.
    c. It was easier for them to move through the snow with their skis on.
    d. They thought the skis would be stolen if they left them in the car.

17. How did Joan and Marty find shelter?
    a. They drove to a house on the road.
    b. They skied to the Mountain Top Hotel.
    c. They smelled smoke from a fireplace.
    d. A police car drove them there.

▲18. After Joan and Marty were safely inside the house, they probably
    a. were glad they hadn't arrived a day earlier.
    b. never went on a ski trip again.
    c. decided to call for a weather report.
    d. went back to get their car.

●19. This story is mainly about
    a. how to read a map and follow directions.
    b. how to get out of a blizzard.
    c. what happened when Joan and Marty went skiing.
    d. Joan and Marty's adventure during a blizzard.

Check your answers with the key.

_____START THE PLAYER_____

●●●●A●●●●

The sky was gray and the dark clouds were heavy with the promise of snow. The sharp, biting winter wind swooped down on the dead leaves and sent them fluttering through the air. As the first white, feathery snowflakes began to fall, a small car drove around the bend in the lonely country road and pulled over to the side.

"You did it again, Joan," Marty shouted angrily at the young woman sitting next to him. "You got us lost again. Can't you read and follow a simple map?"

"Oh, stop squawking," Joan snapped at the young man behind the wheel. "You always shout when you know you're wrong too. I was only trying to keep track of those dumb side roads you insist on taking whenever we go on a ski trip. Besides, whose clever idea was it to go past the DETOUR sign?"

"Okay, you're right," Marty said in a calming voice. "Let's stop arguing. We've got to move on before we're caught in that blizzard the radio weather report told us about."

Joan looked out the car window. "Marty," she cried, "while we've been fighting, the snow has almost covered the front and back windows. Let's head back to the sign."

Marty started the engine. It turned over, grumbled like an old bear disturbed in its sleep, and then died. He tried several times to start it again. Nothing happened.

———START THE PLAYER———

20. **see**   **hear**   **feel**   **taste**   **smell**

a. _____ The sky was gray and the dark clouds were heavy with the promise of snow.

b. _____ The sharp, biting winter wind swooped down on the dead leaves

_____ and sent them fluttering through the air.

c. _____ As the first white, feathery snowflakes began to fall, a small car drove around the bend in the lonely country road and pulled over to the side.

d. _____ "Oh, stop squawking," Joan snapped at the young man behind the wheel.

e. _____ It turned over, grumbled like an old bear disturbed in its sleep, and then died.

———START THE PLAYER———

•••• **B** ••••

"I'll fix it," Marty said as he got out of the car. "It's probably a loose wire. This old heap of metal has never let us down yet."

Joan followed him, biting her lips to keep from saying what both of them knew, that there was something seriously wrong with the little car that had taken them for so many miles of good times. She watched nervously as Marty bent over the engine. The sounds of metal against metal when Marty tapped on the engine's many parts cut through the quiet, icy air like a knife. Suddenly, Marty stood straight up and turned toward her. His face was as white as the snow that dusted the top of his brightly colored cap.

"There's no use trying to fool ourselves, Joan," he said. "Our little car has had it."

"What do we do now?" Joan asked in a whisper so low she hardly knew her own voice. "If we stay in the car and the blizzard continues the way it is now, the car will soon be covered by snow drifts. We'll die here."

"That's no way to talk," Marty said bravely. "We have too much living and skiing to do."

Joan closed her eyes tightly as if to squeeze out an idea that would save them. Then she began brushing the snow from the trunk of the car. The snow was cold and wet. It stuck to her fingers like ice from a freezer. She trembled for a moment as the pain from the cold shot through her body like spear points.

"What are you doing?" Marty shouted over a sudden blast of wind as Joan opened the trunk and dragged out their suitcase.

"We've got to get out of here," she replied. "Here, take these sweaters; we can put them on in the car. Our lives depend on staying warm."

21. **see**   **hear**   **feel**   **taste**   **smell**

a. _____ The sounds of metal against metal when Marty tapped on the

_____ engine's many parts cut through the quiet, icy air like a knife.

b. _____ His face was as white as the snow that dusted the top of his brightly colored cap.

c. _____ "What do we do now?" Joan asked in a whisper so low she hardly knew her own voice.

d. _____ The snow was cold and wet.

e. _____ She trembled for a moment as the pain from the cold shot through her body like spear points.

_____**START THE PLAYER**_____

•••• C ••••

After they had wrapped themselves in the extra clothing, Marty began to laugh loudly. "What's so funny?" Joan muttered.

"You! Me! We must look like two fat Eskimos."

"Never mind the jokes," Joan said, half smiling. "We'll be two, fat, dead Eskimos if we don't get moving before dark. How about some cross-country skiing?" Their hands moved quickly as they put on their skis.

"We can take along the thermos of hot soup that we brought with us," Marty suggested.

"Let's have some before we start out," Joan said as she reached for the thermos and removed the cover. She enjoyed the pleasing flavor of the hot soup. The heat warmed her throat and spread to her insides, readying her for the journey.

Thick and heavy, the cold snow almost blinded them as they made their way along the road. The wind whistled around their ears like a piper calling a deadly tune. Each of them wondered if they would ever find shelter or see another human being again.

Suddenly, Joan pulled at Marty's sleeve. "Do you smell something?" she asked.

"Yes, it's wood burning," he answered. "We must be near a house." They skied on, their noses following the scent of smoking pine logs. Through the curtain of snow they saw a house.

"You people are very lucky you found us," the woman said as she led them to the fireplace. "Heavy snow is expected to fall all night. Where were you headed?"

"To Mountain Top Hotel," Marty answered.

"I guess you didn't hear," the woman said. "That place burned down during the night."

22. **see   hear   feel   taste   smell**

a. _____ She enjoyed the pleasing flavor of the hot soup. The heat warmed

_____ her throat and spread to her insides, readying her for the journey.

b. _____ Thick and heavy, the cold snow almost blinded them as they made

_____ their way along the road.

c. _____ The wind whistled around their ears like a piper calling a deadly tune.

d. _____ They skied on, their noses following the scent of smoking pine logs.

e. _____ Through the curtain of snow they saw a house.

_____START THE PLAYER_____

PRACTICE

Understanding Sensory Images

Directions: Read the story. Then write the correct sense word(s) for each item.

It was one of those clear days when sunlight dances upon the ground and not a cloud goes drifting by. A good day for the World Series to be played. Matt and I were there to see it. Our eyes stayed fixed like anchors on the figures on the diamond and our throats burned like a red-hot furnace from hours of yelling, cheering, groaning. A light breeze stirred the air. The scent of hot food was carried on the breeze. My mouth watered.

"Gee," I said to Matt. "I sure could use a big, juicy hot dog covered with ketchup."

CRACK!

An ear-splitting roar from the crowd attacked our ears as we watched the player run from base to base and slide home in a cloud of dust.

"Wow! What a play!" Matt said. The breeze blew another reminder of hot food. "Hot dog, you said? Get me one too, will you?"

We eyed each other. It was near the end of the game and neither of us was willing to leave our seats. Then Matt spotted a kid and called her over.

"Here's three dollars, kid," Matt said. "Get us two hot dogs with the works on 'em and buy one for yourself."

The kid went galloping off. She came back and handed Matt two dollars. "Sorry," the kid said. She was enjoying a big, fat, juicy hot dog. "They only had my hot dog left."

Matt turned red with anger, but his words were lost in another roar from the crowd.

see	hear	feel	taste	smell

1. _____ It was one of those clear days when sunlight dances upon the ground and not a cloud goes drifting by.

2. _____ Our eyes stayed fixed like anchors on the figures on the diamond and our throats burned like a red-hot furnace from hours of yelling, _____ cheering, groaning.

3. _____ A light breeze stirred the air. The scent of hot food was carried on _____ the breeze.

4. _____ An ear-splitting roar from the crowd attacked our ears as we watched the player run from base to base and slide home in a _____ cloud of dust.

5. _____ She was enjoying a big, fat, juicy hot dog.

6. _____ Matt turned red with anger, but his words were lost in another roar _____ from the crowd.

Check your answers with the key.

Harvest of Tears

——WORD STUDY——

a.	**savage**	Wild and fierce
b.	**prairie**	A large area of flat or rolling land with grass but few or no trees
c.	**ruin**	Destroy or spoil
d.	**settler**	Someone who establishes residence or sets up a home in a place

In the old days, life was not easy for the (1) _____ who lived in

the West. First, he had to travel over miles and miles of

(2) _____, searching for a good place to grow his crops. After the

crops were planted, he would hope that a (3) _____ storm

wouldn't (4) _____ his harvest.

e.	**thirst**	The desire for something to drink
f.	**partner**	Someone with whom you share something, as a business
g.	**rude**	Not polite

My business (5) _____ makes the world's worst coffee. I don't

want to be (6) _____, so I've never told her. Usually, I just don't

drink it. But today I was so thirsty that I was forced to satisfy my

(7) _____ by drinking two cups of the stuff.

h.	**tears**	Drops of salty liquid coming from the eye
i.	**lonesome**	The feeling of being lonely

The woman felt very (8) _____ after her best friend moved away.

When she thought about the good times they had had together,

(9) _____ would form in her eyes.

——START THE PLAYER——

Proper Nouns

Ramon	Arizona	Miss Gonzales
Maria	Juan	Migrant Help Center
Dusty	Carmen	

Harvest of Tears

by Karen Papagapitos

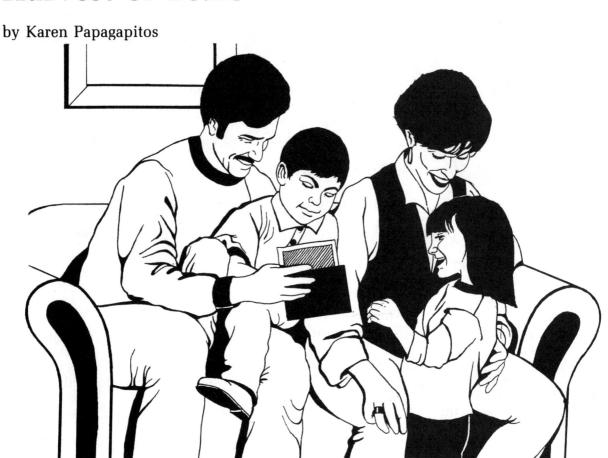

Ramon heard the voices of his children as he pulled into the driveway—his driveway.

If only his mother and father could see him now, they would be so proud. He had made it! He owned a beautiful home, had a great wife, and two beautiful children.

He stepped out of a shiny blue car and walked into the bright, sunny kitchen. "Hi, honey." Ramon kissed his wife Maria. For a moment she looked just like his mother. But there were no lines in Maria's face. Yes, that's what was missing. That, and the threadbare dress his mother wore year after year as she and Ramon worked in the fields.

Answer questions 10 and 11.

10. In what ways was Maria different from Ramon's mother? (Write the letters of **all** the answers.)
   a. She looked nothing like Ramon's mother.
   b. She didn't have lines in her face as Ramon's mother had had.
   c. She was shorter than Ramon's mother.
   d. She didn't wear a threadbare dress as Ramon's mother had.

▲11. Who are the boy and the woman Ramon is thinking about in the picture?
   a. Ramon and his mother
   b. Ramon and Maria
   c. Ramon's son and Ramon's mother
   d. Ramon's son and Maria

_____ **START THE PLAYER** _____

COMPREHENSION CHECK

Directions: Write or circle the letter of your choice.

12. Write the letters of **all** the sentences that tell about Ramon's present life.
    a. Ramon owns a building company.
    b. Ramon's family moves a lot.
    c. Ramon has a wife and two children.
    d. Ramon earns money picking vegetables.
    e. Ramon lives in a nice house.

13. Ramon remembers being thirsty from picking crops and
    a. running away from rude people.
    b. driving on dusty roads.
    c. eating hot food.
    d. living where the weather was hot and dry.

▲14. Ramon liked the idea that his children's friends were staying for dinner because
    a. Maria cooked too much food for his family.
    b. his children didn't make friends easily.
    c. he thought his children's friends were nice kids.
    d. he was glad his children had friends since he never had any when he was a child.

15. Why didn't Ramon ever have a real friend?
    a. His family was always moving.
    b. He was rude and not friendly.
    c. Other children didn't like him.
    d. He didn't go to school.

16. Why did Ramon's mother want him to go to school?
    a. To learn how to pick beans
    b. To make something of himself
    c. Because he was too young to take care of the baby
    d. So people could make fun of him

17. Why did Dusty call Ramon?
    a. To tell him she had closed the deal on the shopping center
    b. To tell him she had found a new partner
    c. To ask if she could come over for dinner
    d. To tell him his idea for the Migrant Help Center had been OK'd

▲18. What kind of person is Ramon?
    a. A selfish person
    b. A greedy person
    c. A person who doesn't like to face up to things
    d. A good person who cares about others

●19. This story is mainly about
    a. what it's like to build shopping centers.
    b. how to harvest crops.
    c. how Ramon's past helped him to help others.
    d. Maria's love for her husband.

Check your answers with the key.

_____START THE PLAYER_____

1 Ramon heard the voices of his children as he pulled into the driveway—his driveway.

If only his mother and father could see him now, they would be so proud. He had made it! He owned a beautiful home, had a great wife, and two beautiful children.

He stepped out of a shiny blue car and walked into the bright, sunny kitchen. "Hi, honey." Ramon kissed his wife Maria. For a moment she looked just like his mother. But there were no lines in Maria's face. Yes, that's what was missing. That, and the threadbare dress his mother wore year after year as she and Ramon worked in the fields.

"How did it go today, Ramon?" Maria handed him a cool glass of ice water.

"Good. Real good. In fact, Dusty and I were able to close the deal on the shopping center in one hour flat." Dusty was Ramon's partner in their building company.

The cool water slid down Ramon's throat and took away the thirst he always had. A savage thirst, like the kind he remembered as a little boy working in the fields of Arizona.

"Momma," he would ask, "isn't there anything to drink?"

"Quiet, boy! You know there isn't until we stop picking these beans. Just keep busy, and you will forget about it!" his mother would answer back while she kept picking.

Even when they weren't picking crops, Ramon remembers being thirsty from the dust of the road. His family would drive over miles and miles of prairie, following the crops that were ready to be picked. They never became settlers in any town. "Couldn't," his father would tell him. "We have to go where the work is. We have to keep moving on."

Ramon's thoughts were broken as Juan and Carmen jumped into his lap. They covered his face with kisses and then ran out to play until dinner was ready.

"Come back in ten minutes," Maria called after them.

"Who's that out there with them?" Ramon asked as he looked in the backyard.

"The Baker twins from school. They're staying for dinner. Is that OK?"

"Sure. You know I like to have the kids bring their friends home."

2 Ramon couldn't remember ever having a friend, a real friend. He would no sooner get to know someone at school when his family would have to move on. But that was the way it was. Always moving on to new places, new schools. Always leaving friends. Always feeling lonesome.

———————START THE PLAYER———————

20. Write **past** if the description tells about Ramon's childhood. Write **present** if the description tells about Ramon's life now. Write **both** if the description tells about both Ramon's childhood and his life now.

a. _____ A crop-picker

b. _____ Always thirsty

c. _____ Never a settler

d. _____ Owner of a beautiful home

e. _____ Lonesome most of the time

f. _____ Poor

g. _____ Owner of a building company

h. _____ Happy with his life

———————START THE PLAYER———————

▲21. How do you think Ramon feels in shaded part 1 of the story?
a. Happy   c. Angered
b. Sad   d. Fearful

▲22. How do you think Ramon feels in shaded part 2 of the story?
a. Very happy   c. Angered
b. Somewhat sad   d. Proud

———————START THE PLAYER———————   ———————START THE PLAYER———————

•••**B**••••

"Why don't you rest before dinner?" Maria said, brushing the hair from his eyes.

Almost instantly Ramon let himself fall into a troubled sleep. Now the pictures of his past were clearer. Ramon was nine again. He was watching his mother get the baby ready to take to the fields with her.

"But, Momma, I don't want to go to school," young Ramon said. "The bossman says it won't do me much good anyhow. I can watch the baby for you, Momma. Please let me stay."

"The baby's going to sleep most of the day, Ramon. That's not what I want you to do. You have a good head on you. You can make something of yourself. But you've got to believe that and work hard trying to learn what you can. This teacher—what's her name?"

"Gonzales."

"This Miss Gonzales, she believes in you. Told me so herself. You've got to go, Ramon. It's your only hope."

"But the other kids laugh, Momma. Sometimes the big folks do too."

"I know, son," Ramon's mother sighed. "But don't let a few rude people ruin your life. They are easier to forget than a harvest of tears year after year."

▲ 23. Write or circle the letters of **all** the sentences that tell about Ramon's mother.
   a. She was selfish.
   b. She was lazy.
   c. She was not selfish.
   d. She loved Ramon.
   e. She hated Ramon.
   f. She wanted Ramon to grow up to be like her.
   g. She wanted Ramon to grow up to have a better life than she had.

▲ 24. What main event in Ramon's past helped him succeed?
   a. His mother let him watch the baby.
   b. His mother didn't let people laugh at him.
   c. His mother made him go to school.
   d. His mother made him work in the fields.

———**START THE PLAYER**———

•••●C●•••

"Ramon, wake up. Dinner's ready." Maria's voice broke into his dream.

"I'll go wash up."

"You were dreaming about the old days again, weren't you?" Maria asked softly.

Ramon nodded silently.

"Won't you ever forget them? We have a new life now."

"I don't want to forget them, Maria. Don't you see . . ."

Just then the phone rang.

"It's for you, Ramon. It's Dusty."

Ramon took the phone from Maria.

"Hi, Dusty. . . . That's wonderful!" Ramon said. "See you tomorrow."

"What is it? Why are you so happy?"

Maria looked at her husband.

"Like I was telling you, Maria, I can't forget the old days. If I do, they will always be there for other people. I've made it, and it's up to me to help change things."

"What are you talking about?"

"Dusty just told me that my idea for a Migrant Help Center has been OK'd. Pickers will be able to get food, medical care, clothing, and housing for their families. It's a dream come true!"

"I see now why you didn't try to forget. I'm so proud, Ramon."

"Like my Momma said, Maria—it's hard to forget a harvest of tears."

_____START THE PLAYER_____

25. Write or circle the letters of **all** the sentences that tell the effects of Ramon's past as a farm worker.
    a. He understands the problems faced by families who work picking crops.
    b. He thinks people who work picking crops have a good life.
    c. He wants to help change things for families who work picking crops.
    d. He wants to build a Migrant Help Center.
    e. He wants his children to work picking crops.

_____START THE PLAYER_____

▲ 26. What is the author's message?
    a. If a person's past is bad, he or she should forget it.
    b. Families who work picking crops don't have such a bad life.
    c. If people who succeed remember their past, they can help change things for others who have the same problems they once did.
    d. People who work picking crops need places to get food, medical care, housing, and clothing.

_____START THE PLAYER_____

PRACTICE

Using a Combination of Skills

Directions: Read the story. Then answer the questions.

One night last summer I was taking a walk with my daughter, Joan. My throat felt like sandpaper, and I had a heavy cough. I was smoking as usual.

"It's time I quit smoking," I said.

"Think you can do it, Mom?" Joan asked.

"It's worth a try," I answered.

The next morning I faced my first test. I was used to having a smoke right after breakfast. But I took out a pack of hard candy instead and popped a piece of candy in my mouth.

On the way to the bus stop it seemed as though everybody I saw was smoking. I felt jumpy.

I was just as jumpy at work. I repair electric motors. You have to have a steady hand for that job. Well, that first morning my hands shook. I drank water and chewed gum to calm myself, but it didn't work. The rest of the day was no better.

At supper, Joan asked, "How did it go?" Joan smoked, and so she knew it was hard for me to stop.

"Not good," I told her, "but I've made it so far."

The next morning things were no better. But after a few weeks, I no longer felt jumpy. Something else happened, too. My cough was gone, and my throat didn't feel rough. I was able to take longer walks without getting tired so quickly. And food tasted better than it had in years. Of course, I was also saving money.

When Joan saw me licking the habit, she decided to try. We kind of helped each other. I'm sure that made it easier for both of us to stop smoking. We both did, too!

Take it from an ex-smoker—a two-pack-a-day smoker—it pays to stop. And I'm not kidding.

1. Write **before** if the description tells about the storyteller before she gave up smoking. Write **after** if the description tells about the storyteller after she gave up smoking. Write **both** if the description tells about the storyteller both before and after she gave up smoking.

   a. _____ Coughed and had a rough throat

   b. _____ Took long walks without getting tired

   c. _____ Repaired electric motors

   d. _____ Saved money

▲ 2. How did the storyteller feel the first day she gave up smoking?
   a. Happy
   b. Nervous
   c. Amused
   d. Tired

3. Write the word **cause** or **effect** to show what each statement is.

   a. _____ Joan decided to give up smoking.

   b. _____ Joan saw her mother licking the habit.

▲ 4. What is the author's message?
   a. Smoking causes heart trouble and other illnesses.
   b. Daughters like to do the same things that their mothers do.
   c. You have to have a steady hand to repair electric motors.
   d. Giving up smoking isn't easy, but you can do it if you really try.

Check your answers with the key.

HOW TO SCORE FOR MASTERY

To evaluate mastery efficiently, the chart below may be used. The percentage scores are then transferred to the record form on the next page.

It is suggested that the teacher use judgment in raising or lowering the mastery criteria when the items in question are more difficult or easier than the "general" level of difficulty of evaluative items in the program.

As a rule, an approximate score of 80% of correct responses is considered to be mastery. Note that the mastery percentage is underlined in the chart below. For example, mastery in a ten-item test is eight right, or 80%.

Number of Items

Right	3	4	5	6	7	8	9	10	11	12	13	14	15	16	17	18	19	20	21	22	23	24	25	26	27	28	29	30
1	33	25	20	17	14	13	11	10	9	8	8	7	7	6	6	5	5	5	5	5	4	4	4	4	4	4	3	3
2	66	50	40	33	29	25	22	20	18	17	15	14	13	13	12	11	11	10	9	9	9	8	8	8	7	7	7	7
3	100	75	60	50	43	38	33	30	27	25	23	21	20	19	18	17	16	15	14	14	13	13	12	12	11	11	10	10
4		100	80	67	57	50	44	40	36	33	31	29	27	25	24	22	21	20	19	18	17	17	16	15	15	14	14	13
5			100	83	72	63	56	50	45	42	38	36	33	31	29	28	26	25	24	23	22	21	20	19	19	18	17	17
6				100	86	75	67	60	55	50	46	43	40	38	35	33	32	30	29	27	26	25	24	23	22	21	21	20
7					100	88	78	70	64	58	54	50	47	44	41	39	37	35	33	32	30	29	28	27	26	25	24	23
8						100	89	80	73	67	62	57	53	50	47	44	42	40	38	36	35	33	32	31	30	29	28	27
9							100	90	82	75	69	64	60	56	53	50	47	45	43	41	39	38	36	35	33	32	31	30
10								100	91	83	77	71	67	63	59	56	53	50	48	45	43	42	40	39	37	36	34	33
11									100	92	85	79	73	69	65	61	58	55	52	50	48	46	44	42	41	39	38	37
12										100	92	86	80	75	71	67	63	60	57	55	52	50	48	46	44	43	41	40
13											100	93	87	81	76	72	68	65	62	59	57	54	52	50	48	46	44	43
14												100	93	88	82	78	74	70	67	64	61	58	56	54	52	50	48	47
15													100	94	87	83	79	75	71	68	65	63	60	58	56	54	52	50
16														100	94	89	84	80	76	73	70	67	64	62	59	57	55	53
17															100	94	89	85	81	77	74	71	68	65	63	61	59	57
18																100	95	90	86	82	78	75	72	69	67	64	62	60
19																	100	95	91	86	83	79	76	73	70	68	65	63
20																		100	95	91	87	83	80	77	74	72	69	67
21																			100	95	91	88	84	81	78	75	72	70
22																				100	96	92	88	85	81	79	76	73
23																					100	96	92	88	85	82	79	77
24																						100	96	92	89	86	83	80
25																							100	96	93	89	86	83
26																								100	96	93	89	87
27																									100	96	93	90
28																										100	96	93
29																											100	97
30																												100

Number of Items Right (row labels)

PROGRESS CHART

Reading Strategies DA

Name _____

Lesson Number	Date	Word Study Score	Preview and Comprehension Check Score	Skill Instruction Score	Lesson Mastered	Practice Assigned	Practice Mastered
1							
2							
3							
4							
5							
6							
7							
8							
9							
10							
11							
12							
13							
14							
15							
16							
17							
18							
19							
20							

This page may be reproduced for school use.

DA-1

Word Study
1. frozen
2. curiosity
3. commanded
4. attention
5. neighborhood
6. weave
7. realize
8. purpose
9. familiar
10. future

Preview
11. b
12. d

Comprehension Check
13. b
▲ 14. d
15. b
▲ 16. a
17. d
18. c
19. c
● 20. b

Skill Instruction
21. d
22. b
23. a
24. c
25. d
26. a
27. b
28. d
29. b
30. c

Practice
1. a
2. d
3. d
4. a
5. c
6. b

DA-2

Word Study
1. habit
2. argue
3. agree
4. business
5. patiently
6. hesitate
7. razor
8. possession
9. jail

Preview
10. b
11. a
12. d

Comprehension Check
13. b
14. d
15. a
▲ 16. d
▲ 17. c
18. c
19. a
● 20. d

Skill Instruction
21. Joe Palmer, beard
22. 1700s
23. forties, Fitchburg
24. fight
25. four
† brush, soap, razor, knife
26. a year
27. growing a beard, fighting
28. jailer, his men, chair
29. Philadelphia, New York
30. Lincoln, Lee
† 31. 1870s, 1880s

Practice
1. great-grandfather, the United States
2. 1863, farmer, Hunan Province
3. 1864; San Francisco, California; railroad
4. 1890; oldest; St. Louis, Missouri; market
5. three, youngest
6. 19, 1910, doctor
7. grandfather, father, doctors

† The answers may appear in any order.

Answer Key

DA-3

Word Study
1. person
2. life jacket
3. support
4. nature
5. alligator
6. dangerous
7. nurse
8. level
9. appearance

Preview
10. b
11. c

Comprehension Check
12. d
▲13. c
14. d
15. a
▲16. c
17. a
18. a
● 19. d

Skill Instruction
● 20. a
● 21. c
● 22. d
● 23. b
● 24. c
● 25. a
● 26. d

Practice
● 1. c
● 2. a
● 3. b
● 4. d

DA-4

Word Study
1. champion
2. national
3. popular
4. distance
5. problem
6. language
7. control
8. upset
9. mystery

Preview
10. c
11. d

Skill Instruction
12. b
13. c
14. a
▲15. c
16. c
17. b
▲18. d
19. b
† 20. a, d
▲21. b

Comprehension Check
22. c
23. b
24. b
25. a
26. c
▲27. b
28. d
29. c
30. a
● 31. d

Practice
1. d
▲ 2. c
3. d
▲ 4. a
▲ 5. c

DA-5

Word Study
1. condition
2. develop
3. program
4. strength
5. rise
6. immediately
7. hostage
8. avoid
9. tear gas
10. defend

Preview
11. b
12. d

Comprehension Check
13. d
14. c
▲ 15. d
▲ 16. a
17. a
18. d
19. b
● 20. a

Skill Instruction
● 21. c
22. 1. g
    2. h
    3. e
    4. b
    5. d
    6. f
    7. c
    8. a
● 23. b
24. 1. d
    2. e
    3. g
    4. f
    5. i
    6. b
    7. h
    8. a
    9. c
● 25. d
26. 1. i
    2. d
    3. b
    4. f
    5. h
    6. g
    7. a
    8. c
    9. e

Practice
● 1. c
2. 1. e
   2. g
   3. d
   4. c
   5. f
   6. a
   7. b

† The answers may appear in any order.

144

DA-6

Word Study
1. boss
2. silence
3. union
4. creature
5. peaceful
6. dozen
7. cheerful
8. ghost
9. vanish

Preview
† 10. a, c, d
▲ 11. a

Comprehension Check
† 12. b, c, d
13. c
† 14. a, c, e
▲ 15. a
16. d
▲ 17. b
18. b
● 19. c

Skill Instruction
20. a. 4
b. 2
c. 5
d. 3
e. 1
f. 6

21. a. 1
b. 5
c. 2
d. 4
e. 3

22. a. 3
b. 4
c. 2
d. 5
e. 1

23. a. 4
b. 1
c. 3
d. 2
e. 5

24. a. 2
b. 4
c. 3
d. 5
e. 1

Practice
1. a. 4
b. 2
c. 1
d. 5
e. 3

2. a. 3
b. 2
c. 6
d. 4
e. 1
f. 5

DA-7

Word Study
1. surgery
2. bullet
3. stomach
4. examine
5. wound
6. pain
7. eyelid
8. health
9. medicine

Preview
▲ 10. c
† 11. b, c, d

Comprehension Check
12. b
13. b
14. b
15. d
▲ 16. c
▲ 17. d
18. c
● 19. b

Skill Instruction
20. a. cause
b. effect
21. a. effect
b. cause
22. 1. Thousands of dollars and gold dust changed hands.
2. Everybody went home.
23. a. cause
b. effect
24. a. effect
b. cause
† 25. b, d
26. a. cause
b. effect
27. c
† 28. a, e

Practice
1. a. cause
b. effect
† 2. a, b, d, f
† 3. b, c, e
4. a. effect
b. cause

†The answers may appear in any order.

145

Answer Key

DA-8

Word Study

1. million
2. dinosaur
3. scores
4. ton
5. arrangement
6. area
7. pause
8. improve
9. perform
10. talon

Preview

† 11. a, b, d
▲ 12. b

Comprehension Check

13. d
14. b
▲ 15. c
16. c
17. a
18. c
19. a
● 20. d

Skill Instruction

21.

		Dromaeosaurus	Tyrannosaurus
a.	Where it lived:	North America	North America
b.	When it lived:	late Cretaceous times	late Cretaceous times
c.	Length from nose to tail:	about 9 feet	about 50 feet
d.	How tall it was:	5 or 6 feet	18½ feet
e.	Weight:	about 100 pounds	6 - 8 tons
f.	Number of legs:	2	2
g.	Had talons:	yes	yes
h.	Speed:	fast	slow
i.	Number of fingers on each hand:	3	2
j.	Use of arms and hands:	catch and hold onto game	raise itself from the ground

22. Tyrannosaurus
† 23. a, b, e, f
24. Dromaeosaurus
25. Dromaeosaurus
26. Tyrannosaurus
27. Tyrannosaurus

Practice

		Bob Peterson	Jackie Brown
1. a.	Finished high school:	yes	yes
b.	Had good work habits:	yes	yes
c.	Number of years at same kind of work:	4	6
d.	Smiled a lot:	no	yes

† 2. a, b
3. Jackie
4. Jackie
5. Jackie

† The answers may appear in any order.

Answer Key

DA-9

Word Study
1. report
2. earthquake
3. scientific
4. telescope
5. news
6. explode
7. newspaper
8. hint
9. customer
10. burst

Preview
▲ 11. c
▲ 12. d

Comprehension Check
13. a
14. c
15. b, e
† 16. a, c, d, e, h
▲ 17. d
18. a
19. c
● 20. c

Skill Instruction
21. a, c, g
22. a, c, f, g, h
23. d, e, g

Practice
1. a, c, e, f, g, i

DA-10

Word Study
1. nineteen
2. flight
3. protect
4. interrupt
5. suggest
6. treat
7. zero
8. protection

Preview
9. a
▲ 10. c

Skill Instruction
▲ 11. b
▲ 12. a
▲ 13. b
▲ 14. d
▲ 15. a
▲ 16. d
▲ 17. b
▲ 18. c
▲ 19. b
▲ 20. a
▲ 21. c

Comprehension Check
22. c
23. d
▲ 24. a
25. b
▲ 26. b
27. d
▲ 28. b
● 29. c

Practice
▲ 1. d
▲ 2. b
▲ 3. b
▲ 4. a

† The answers may appear in any order.

Answer Key

DA-11

Word Study
1. claws
2. tame
3. difficult
4. weary
5. insist
6. helmet
7. steady
8. gravity
9. human

Preview
▲ 10. c
▲ 11. a

Comprehension Check
12. b
▲ 13. a
▲ 14. b
▲ 15. c
† 16. b, d, e
▲ 17. b
18. d
● 19. b

Skill Instruction*
20. One evening in 1837
21. London at Jane Alsop's house
22. After 1845
23. Different parts of London
24. The 1860s and 1870s
25. In the country
26. One summer day in 1877
27. An army post near Aldershot
28. 1877
29. Newport
30. The middle of the day in 1904
31. Liverpool

Practice*
1. In the afternoon
2. In the newsroom of the *New City News*
3. In the winter
4. On Main Street
5. Almost morning
6. At the hospital

DA-12

Word Study
1. nervous
2. court
3. jail
4. freedom
5. fist
6. suspect
7. accuse
8. uneasy
9. shove
10. dignity

Preview
11. c
† 12. b, c, e

Comprehension Check
13. a
14. b
15. d
16. b
17. c
▲ 18. d
19. a
● 20. d

Skill Instruction
▲ 21. a
▲ 22. d
▲ 23. b
24. b
25. d
26. c
27. d
▲ 28. a
▲ 29. b
30. c
▲ 31. a
▲ 32. c

Practice
▲ 1. c
▲ 2. a
▲ 3. d
▲ 4. b
▲ 5. c

---

† The answers may appear in any order.
* The answers may be worded differently. Check with your teacher.

Answer Key

DA-13

Word Study	Comprehension Check	Skill Instruction	Practice
1. dull	11. d	19. a. 5	1. a. 3
2. honest	12. b	b. 2	b. 5
3. movie	† 13. a, c, d, e, f	c. 7	c. 1
4. character	14. a	d. 3	d. 2
5. stunt	15. c	e. 1	e. 4
6. action	16. c, d, e	f. 6	▲ 2. d
7. actor	▲ 17. b	g. 4	▲ 3. a
8. cast	● 18. a	▲ 20. c	▲ 4. c
Preview		†▲ 21. b, e	
9. d		▲ 22. d	
10. b		▲ 23. a	

DA-14

Word Study	Comprehension Check	Skill Instruction	Practice
1. torn	13. d	† 21. a, c, f	† 1. a, c
2. remind	14. c	† 22. c, d, g	2. e
3. medal	15. b	† 23. e, f	
4. Colonel	16. a		
5. motion	17. c		
6. jeep	▲ 18. d		
7. soldier	▲ 19. a		
8. position	● 20. c		
9. rifle			
10. eighteen			
Preview			
▲ 11. d			
▲ 12. b			

DA-15

Word Study	Skill Instruction	Comprehension Check	Practice
1. October	† 11. b, d	21. d	1. b
2. bushel	12. c	▲ 22. c	†▲ 2. a, b, d, e
3. anger	13. a	▲ 23. b	▲ 3. c
4. drugs	14. b	24. c	▲ 4. d
5. responsible	† 15. b, c, e	25. a	
6. afford	16. c	26. a	
7. expensive	▲ 17. d	▲ 27. b	
8. future	18. b	● 28. d	
Preview	▲ 19. a		
9. b	▲ 20. b		
▲ 10. d			

† The answers may appear in any order.

DA-16

Word Study
1. crew
2. neighborhood
3. credit
4. tide
5. shallow
6. stern
7. bare
8. ad
9. toothpaste
10. product

Preview
11. c
12. a. need
    b. better
    c. think

Comprehension Check
13. b
▲ 14. a
▲ 15. d
▲ 16. b
17. a
18. c
19. d
▲ 20. a
● 21. c.

Skill Instruction
22. b
23. c
24. a
25. a
26. d
27. d
28. e

Practice
1. b
2. e
3. a
4. c
5. d

DA-17

Word Study
1. blizzard
2. temperature
3. icy
4. adapt
5. Eskimo
6. northern
7. polar
8. zone

Preview
9. d
▲ 10. c

Comprehension Check
11. b
12. c
▲ 13. b
14. a
15. a
16. d
† 17. b, c, e, f, g
18. c

Skill Instruction
▲ 19. a
20. d
21. c
22. c
23. b
▲ 24. d

Practice
1. d
2. a
▲ 3. c
▲ 4. b

DA-18

Word Study
1. warrior
2. anger
3. battle
4. jungle
5. stress
6. respond
7. decision
8. friendship
9. companion
10. dignity

Preview
▲ 11. a
12. c

Comprehension Check
13. a
14. b
15. d
▲ 16. c
17. a
18. a
▲ 19. c
● 20. c

Skill Instruction
21. a. opinion
    b. fact
    c. opinion
    d. fact
    e. opinion
    f. fact
22. a. opinion
    b. fact
    c. opinion
    d. fact
    e. opinion
23. a. fact
    b. fact
    c. fact
    d. opinion
    e. opinion
24. a. opinion
    b. fact

Practice
1. fact
2. opinion
3. fact
4. opinion
5. opinion
6. opinion
7. fact

† The answers may appear in any order.

Answer Key

DA-19

Word Study
1. grumble
2. disturb
3. flutter
4. swoop
5. squawk
6. ski
7. detour
8. mutter
9. thermos

Preview
10. d
▲ 11. c

Comprehension Check
12. c
13. b
14. a
▲ 15. d
16. c
17. c
▲ 18. a
● 19. d

Skill Instruction
20. a. see
† b. feel, see
   c. see
   d. hear
   e. hear
† 21. a. hear, feel
   b. see
   c. hear
   d. feel
   e. feel
† 22. a. taste, feel
†   b. see, feel
   c. hear
   d. smell
   e. see

Practice
1. see
† 2. see, feel
† 3. feel, smell
† 4. hear, see
5. taste
† 6. see, hear

DA-20

Word Study
1. settler
2. prairie
3. savage
4. ruin
5. partner
6. rude
7. thirst
8. lonesome
9. tears

Preview
† 10. b, d
▲ 11. a

Comprehension Check
† 12. a, c, e
13. b
▲ 14. d
15. a
16. b
17. d
▲ 18. d
● 19. c

Skill Instruction
20. a. past
   b. both
   c. past
   d. present
   e. past
   f. past
   g. present
   h. present
▲ 21. a
▲ 22. b
†▲ 23. c, d, g
▲ 24. c
† 25. a, c, d
▲ 26. c

Practice
1. a. before
   b. after
   c. both
   d. after
▲ 2. b
3. a. effect
   b. cause
▲ 4. d

† The answers may appear in any order.

Vocabulary Review

The vocabulary reviews that follow should be used after the completion of each cycle to insure that you know the meaning of each of the cycle words.

Number your paper to match the number of questions in the review. Choose the correct meaning for each word, and then write the letter for your choice on your answer sheet. Use the Answer Key on pages 174 and 175 to check your work.

Choose the best answer.

1. Joe's mother **commanded** him to clean his room. She
   a. ordered Joe to clean his room.
   b. asked Joe if he wanted to clean his room.
   c. told Joe to stop cleaning.
   d. said Joe could clean his room tomorrow.

2. I read the letter out of **curiosity**. I wanted to
   a. know what it said.
   b. mail it.
   c. read it a second time.
   d. throw it away.

3. If my feet feel **frozen**, I should
   a. put on a hat.
   b. go swimming.
   c. go for a walk.
   d. put on socks.

4. Raul paid **attention** to the teacher. This means he
   a. gave the teacher his lunch money.
   b. smiled at the teacher.
   c. listened carefully to the teacher.
   d. started talking.

5. If you are in your **neighborhood**, you are
   a. on a trip.
   b. far from home.
   c. near your home.
   d. in a different town.

6. Which of these might **weave** in and out?
   a. a car going down a winding road
   b. a cat sitting in a tree
   c. a person reading a book
   d. a child sleeping quietly

7. If a song is **familiar**, it is
   a. well known.
   b. pretty.
   c. long.
   d. hard to play.

8. If Marie is thinking about the **future**, she is probably thinking about
   a. what happened last week.
   b. what happened at school yesterday.
   c. what happened today.
   d. what will happen next year.

9. Which is an example of a **purpose**?
   a. I plan to climb that mountain.
   b. I like to climb mountains.
   c. I never climb mountains.
   d. I might climb a mountain.

10. I **realize** that you are going to the movies. That means I
    a. want to go with you.
    b. ask if you are going.
    c. know you are going.
    d. want you to go.

Check your answers with the key.

Choose the best answer.

1. If we both **agree** to meet at the park,
   a. you will go there but I will not.
   b. I will go there but you will not.
   c. both of us say we will be there.
   d. neither of us will be there.

2. Joe likes to **argue** with everyone. He likes to
   a. meet people.
   b. hit people.
   c. talk to people.
   d. disagree with people.

3. How much money I have is none of your **business**. That means
   a. it is not something you need to know.
   b. I want to tell you how much money I have.
   c. you know how much money I have.
   d. you do not give me any money.

4. Someone who has a **habit** of buying books
   a. buys only books about sports.
   b. buys books regularly.
   c. does not like to read.
   d. never buys books.

5. If you **hesitate** before you jump off the diving board, you are probably
   a. tired.
   b. afraid.
   c. hot.
   d. brave.

6. Al **patiently** rocked the crying baby. How did Al rock the baby?
   a. Angrily
   b. Calmly
   c. Quickly
   d. Gladly

7. People who go to **jail** are people who
   a. break laws.
   b. make laws.
   c. study laws.
   d. read the laws.

8. Which of these can be a valuable **possession**?
   a. The sky
   b. The ocean
   c. A house
   d. A nation

9. Max used the **razor** to
   a. chop wood.
   b. cut his beard.
   c. plant seeds.
   d. open the door.

Check your answers with the key.

Choose the best answer.

1. Where would you wear a **life jacket**?
   a. In a car
   b. In the house
   c. In the rain
   d. In a boat

2. Which of these is a **person**?
   a. A woman
   b. A tree
   c. A puppy
   d. A group

3. Which would need **support**?
   a. A plate on the table
   b. A person who cannot walk well
   c. A pot on the stove
   d. A boat in the water

4. Where would you find an **alligator**?
   a. Under the ground
   b. In a river
   c. On top of a mountain
   d. In the sky

5. It can be **dangerous** if a young child
   a. eats dinner.
   b. goes to bed late.
   c. wakes up too early.
   d. climbs a ladder.

6. It is not my **nature** to tell lies. That means
   a. I always tell lies.
   b. I like to tell lies.
   c. I never tell lies.
   d. I cannot help telling lies.

7. Shara did not like the car's **appearance**. That means she did not like
   a. the way the car looked.
   b. the price of the car.
   c. how fast the car went.
   d. the sound of the horn.

8. If the floor is **level**, it is
   a. made from wood.
   b. flat and even.
   c. long.
   d. uneven.

9. A **nurse** would most likely work
   a. in a library.
   b. on a boat.
   c. in a theater.
   d. in a hospital.

Check your answers with the key.

Choose the best answer.

1. A swimming **champion** is someone who
   a. is learning how to swim.
   b. is afraid to swim.
   c. has won first place.
   d. teaches people to swim.

2. A **national** law is a law of a
   a. nation.
   b. state.
   c. city.
   d. town.

3. Ms. Jackson was voted the most **popular** teacher. That means she
   a. was not well liked.
   b. was very well liked.
   c. worked the hardest.
   d. worked longer hours.

4. If I hear a voice in the **distance,** the voice is
   a. in my house.
   b. in my mind.
   c. near me.
   d. far away.

5. If your **language** is different from mine, I probably
   a. come from your town.
   b. cannot understand you.
   c. know exactly what you mean.
   d. have different color hair.

6. If Marisa has a **problem** doing her homework, she
   a. has trouble doing it.
   b. has time to do it.
   c. has to do it tomorrow.
   d. has to show someone how to do it.

7. The student driver lost **control** of the car. That means she
   a. lost the keys.
   b. ran out of gas.
   c. got lost.
   d. could not stop.

8. If you watch a **mystery** movie, you will probably be
   a. laughing.
   b. crying.
   c. wondering what will happen.
   d. singing along.

9. My mother was **upset** because
   a. I passed the test.
   b. I broke the window.
   c. dinner was ready.
   d. the sun was shining.

Check your answers with the key.

Choose the best answer.

1. When I went to the play a woman gave me a **program**. She gave me
   a. a ticket.
   b. a list of the people who put on the play.
   c. a seat.
   d. something to eat.

2. Plants **develop** from seeds means that plants
   a. are the same as seeds.
   b. are bigger than seeds.
   c. grow from seeds.
   d. are taken from seeds.

3. When Martha asked about my **condition**, she was asking me
   a. how I was feeling.
   b. how my family was.
   c. if I could go out.
   d. if I had any questions.

4. If Emily does not have the **strength** to lift the box, she
   a. does not have the time to do it.
   b. does not know how to do it.
   c. is not strong enough to do it.
   d. is not small enough to do it.

5. If Mark does not want to **rise** out of bed, he
   a. does not want to get out of bed.
   b. does not want to stay in bed.
   c. does not want to make his bed.
   d. does not want to take a nap.

6. I **immediately** went home. When did I go home?
   a. Yesterday
   b. Last week
   c. Right away
   d. I did not go home.

7. He wanted to **avoid** the big dog across the street. He wanted to
   a. pet it.
   b. catch it.
   c. weigh it.
   d. keep away from it.

8. The soldiers were commanded to **defend** the town. They were told to
   a. protect the town.
   b. burn down the town.
   c. keep away from the town.
   d. move in to the town.

9. If **tear gas** is thrown near you, you
   a. will see better.
   b. will have trouble seeing.
   c. will hear better.
   d. will have trouble hearing.

10. Which of these would take a **hostage**?
    a. An enemy
    b. A worker
    c. A teacher
    d. A baker

Check your answers with the key.

Choose the best answer.

1. Someone who wants to **silence** a group would want
   a. to keep the group from doing or saying something.
   b. to help the group grow.
   c. to join the group.
   d. to leave the group.

2. Who would join a **union**?
   a. A child
   b. A worker
   c. A coward
   d. An outlaw

3. Which of the following can a **boss** do?
   a. Make you well
   b. Clean your clothes
   c. Fire you
   d. Fix your teeth

4. Which of these is a **creature**?
   a. A rock
   b. A tree
   c. The sky
   d. A bird

5. Which of these is usually sold by the **dozen**?
   a. Books
   b. Eggs
   c. Clothes
   d. Candy

6. Which of the following would make you feel **peaceful**?
   a. Watching a beautiful sunset
   b. Losing your job
   c. Being chased by someone
   d. Failing a test

7. If you are **cheerful**, you are
   a. sad.
   b. scared.
   c. happy.
   d. angry.

8. The quickest way to make food **vanish** is
   a. to make it too salty.
   b. to forget to wrap it well.
   c. to not cook it enough.
   d. to put it in front of hungry people.

9. If you saw a **ghost,** you would most likely be
   a. frightened.
   b. amused.
   c. angry.
   d. calm.

Check your answers with the key.

Choose the best answer.

1. Which of the following would use a **bullet**?
   a. A gun
   b. A car
   c. A stove
   d. A razor

2. What does your **stomach** do for you?
   a. It helps you run.
   b. It helps you think.
   c. It holds your food after you swallow it.
   d. It helps you see better.

3. Which of the following is most likely to do **surgery**?
   a. A champion
   b. A doctor
   c. A soldier
   d. A king

4. I got a **wound** when I
   a. bought some bread.
   b. cut my finger.
   c. fell asleep.
   d. listened to a record.

5. The nurse **examined** the cut on my finger. He
   a. asked me how it happened.
   b. called my mother.
   c. touched my finger.
   d. looked at the cut very carefully.

6. Your **eyelid** is the part that
   a. gets smaller in bright light.
   b. opens and closes over your eye.
   c. has color.
   d. is a bony area above your eye.

7. Someone who is in a lot of **pain** would be most likely to
   a. cry.
   b. laugh.
   c. sing.
   d. eat.

8. When are you most likly to need **medicine**?
   a. When you go to school
   b. When you are sick
   c. When it is early in the morning
   d. When it is very cold outside

9. One way for you to stay in good **health** is to
   a. take care of other people.
   b. get a good job.
   c. take care of your body.
   d. sleep less and eat more.

Check your answers with the key.

Choose the best answer.

1. If you have **scores** of books, you have
   a. many books.
   b. no books.
   c. few books.
   d. two books.

2. Which weighs over a **ton**?
   a. A man
   b. A bicycle
   c. A car
   d. A dog

3. One **million** is
   a. 10,000
   b. 100,000
   c. 1,000,000
   d. 1,000,000,000

4. A **dinosaur** is an animal that
   a. can be found in zoos.
   b. no longer lives on the earth.
   c. eats only plants.
   d. lives in the sea.

5. If you're told to stay in this **area**, then you should stay
   a. out of town.
   b. in your room.
   c. in this place.
   d. in the car.

6. Why might I **pause**?
   a. To look both ways before crossing the street
   b. To get my work done on time
   c. To come in first in a race
   d. To make money

7. If you completed the **arrangement** of your papers, then you
   a. gave away your papers.
   b. copied your papers.
   c. put your papers in order.
   d. sold your papers.

8. What would you **perform**?
   a. Your job
   b. Your parents
   c. Your pet
   d. Your car

9. Where would you find a **talon**?
   a. On a man
   b. On a horse
   c. On a car
   d. On some birds

10. If you **improve** your marks, then you get
   a. higher marks.
   b. lower marks.
   c. the same marks.
   d. no marks.

Check your answers with the key.

Choose the best answer.

1. Which of these would give a **report**?
   a. A clown
   b. A painting
   c. A magic show
   d. A student

2. What happens during an **earthquake**?
   a. The ground moves and shakes.
   b. Everything is calm.
   c. Plants grow quicker.
   d. The earth moves closer to the sun.

3. You would use a **telescope** in order to
   a. see things that are nearby.
   b. see things that are far away.
   c. call someone who is far away.
   d. hear things more clearly.

4. Which of the following is a **scientific** idea?
   a. Plants need light and water to grow.
   b. I like to plant seeds.
   c. Sunflower seeds taste good.
   d. Roses smell nice.

5. If you thought something was going to **explode**
   you would most likely
   a. get close to it.
   b. touch it.
   c. run away from it.
   d. paint it.

6. Larry wanted to hear the **news**. He wanted to
   a. know what just happened.
   b. know what happened a hundred years ago.
   c. listen to a ball game.
   d. listen to the birds sing.

7. You would read a **newspaper** in order to find
   out
   a. how to get to a friend's house.
   b. who won yesterday's election.
   c. who was President in 1888.
   d. how to set a broken bone.

8. Which of these would most likely make me
   feel as though I will **burst**?
   a. Going for a short walk
   b. Taking a short nap
   c. Reading a boring book
   d. Eating too much for dinner

9. Which of these is a **hint**?
   a. I want a new coat for my birthday.
   b. That coat would make a great present!
   c. That coat is red.
   d. Do you sell coats?

10. Where would you be most likely to find a
    customer?
    a. On the beach
    b. In a library
    c. On a boat
    d. In a store

Check your answers with the key.

Choose the best answer.

1. I just bought a ticket for my **flight**. I am going to
   a. see a play.
   b. go on a plane.
   c. drive in a car.
   d. stay home.

2. Someone who is **nineteen** is most likely
   a. a baby.
   b. learning how to ride a bike.
   c. going to college.
   d. very old.

3. If I want to **protect** my skin from the sun, I want to
   a. stay out in the sun for a long time.
   b. get a sunburn.
   c. keep my skin from getting a burn.
   d. drink lots of water.

4. If you **interrupt** me while I am talking, you
   a. start to talk at the same time.
   b. wait until I finish talking before you begin.
   c. never talk to me.
   d. are too shy to talk.

5. If I **suggest** that we take a walk, I might say:
   a. We have to take a walk.
   b. Do you feel like taking a walk?
   c. Did you buy new walking shoes?
   d. I'm too tired to go for a walk.

6. If I **treat** my mother like a child, I would most likely
   a. tell her how nice she looks.
   b. tell her that I know what is best for her.
   c. ask her if she would like to go to the movies.
   d. invite her over for dinner.

7. If you come to me for **protection**, you want me to
   a. keep you safe.
   b. give you some clothes.
   c. give you a ride.
   d. give you a job.

8. When it is below **zero** outside,
   a. I wear a light jacket.
   b. it is nice to go on a picnic.
   c. I try to stay indoors.
   d. it is time to take out the summer clothes.

Check your answers with the key.

Choose the best answer.

1. Which of these would have sharp **claws?**
   a. A razor
   b. A knife
   c. A lion
   d. A snake

2. He thought the job was too **difficult.** That means the job
   a. was too easy.
   b. was too hard.
   c. paid too much.
   d. paid too little.

3. Which of these animals is most likely to be **tame?**
   a. An alligator
   b. A lion
   c. A dog
   d. A hawk

4. After shopping all day I was **weary.** This means
   a. I bought a lot of things.
   b. I was happy.
   c. I spent too much money.
   d. I was tired.

5. If I **insist** that we buy a new car, I am telling you that
   a. it would be nice to buy a new car.
   b. we are going to buy a new car.
   c. we should think about buying a new car.
   d. maybe we should buy a used car.

6. Which of these is most likely to wear a **helmet?**
   a. A student
   b. A teacher
   c. A soldier
   d. A nurse

7. I am looking for a **steady** job. This means I want a job that
   a. has regular days and hours.
   b. has long hours.
   c. needs me to work once in a while.
   d. has hours that change.

8. Which of these is **human?**
   a. A dog
   b. A baby
   c. A cloud
   d. Water

9. Because there is no **gravity** in space,
   a. people can float.
   b. people can run faster.
   c. people can see better.
   d. people can hear more.

Check your answers with the key.

Choose the best answer.

1. Which of these would be a reason to go to **court**?
   a. You broke the law.
   b. You were late for work.
   c. You got a low grade on a test.
   d. You went to sleep early.

2. Which of these is an example of **freedom**?
   a. I always have to do everything my mother says.
   b. I can say and do whatever I want.
   c. I do whatever my friends tell me to do.
   d. I do not know what I want to do.

3. In a **jail** you would most likely find
   a. open doors.
   b. fancy food.
   c. windows with bars.
   d. all of your possessions.

4. My daughter says that tests make her **nervous.** This means that they made her feel
   a. glad.
   b. angry.
   c. upset.
   d. tired.

5. If someone took my money and I **accuse** you, that means I
   a. ask you to help me get it back.
   b. ask you to call the police.
   c. say that you took it.
   d. tell you that I do not know who took it.

6. You would make a **fist** with your
   a. hand.
   b. foot.
   c. head.
   d. mouth.

7. After the bank was robbed, the police said that they had a **suspect.** This means that the police
   a. got all the money back.
   b. thought they knew who robbed the bank.
   c. had no idea who robbed the bank.
   d. were on their way to the bank.

8. If a person acts with **dignity,** that person
   a. does not know how to act.
   b. does not like to act.
   c. always makes other people angry.
   d. wins the respect of others.

9. At the playground children sometimes **shove** each other. This means that they
   a. smile at each other.
   b. play with each other.
   c. yell at each other.
   d. push each other.

10. If I am out walking late at night I often feel **uneasy.** That means that I
    a. wish I could stay out all night.
    b. feel uncomfortable.
    c. feel tired.
    d. want to walk alone.

Check your answers with the key.

Choose the best answer.

1. If the book I am reading is **dull**, I will probably
   a. tell all my friends to read it.
   b. read it again.
   c. stop reading it.
   d. burst out laughing.

2. If you are an **honest** person, people will
   a. talk about you behind your back.
   b. trust you.
   c. never give you a job.
   d. want to take your picture.

3. My friend is a **character** in the play I saw today. My friend is
   a. watching the play.
   b. writing the play.
   c. a person in the play.
   d. writing about the play.

4. When I go to a **movie**, I like to
   a. watch the sun set.
   b. read a book.
   c. do some shopping.
   d. watch the story and eat popcorn.

5. If you can do a **stunt**, you
   a. do not know what you are doing.
   b. are doing something for the first time.
   c. are doing something that is very difficult.
   d. are doing something that everyone knows how to do.

6. I like shows with plenty of **action**. This means I like shows that
   a. have a lot happening in them.
   b. have a lot of singing.
   c. are from another country.
   d. are very funny.

7. You would **not** find an **actor** in
   a. a play.
   b. the movies.
   c. a TV show.
   d. a math book.

8. After the play, there was a party for the **cast**. The party was for
   a. all the people in the play.
   b. only the men in the play.
   c. everyone watching the play.
   d. everyone who liked the play.

Check your answers with the key.

Choose the best answer.

1. Who would be most likely to get a **medal**?
   a. Someone who lost a race
   b. Someone who is arrested for driving too fast
   c. Someone who won a race
   d. Someone who is going to learn how to drive

2. I have to **remind** him to take his medicine. This means that I have to
   a. take his medicine.
   b. buy his medicine.
   c. make sure he does not take any medicine.
   d. tell him so he remembers to take his medicine.

3. If my skirt is **torn**, it
   a. is long.
   b. has holes.
   c. is too short.
   d. is new.

4. A **colonel** is someone who most likely
   a. is thinking about joining the army.
   b. has a very important job in the army.
   c. does not have an important job in the army.
   d. has just joined the army.

5. A **jeep** is a kind of
   a. car.
   b. noise.
   c. clock.
   d. house.

6. The **motion** of the boat made me feel sick. I felt sick because
   a. of the way the boat was moving in the water.
   b. there were too many people on the boat.
   c. it was too hot to be out in a boat.
   d. the boat was making too much noise.

7. **Eighteen** dollars is enough to buy
   a. a house.
   b. a piece of gum.
   c. a car.
   d. a shirt.

8. When the army moved into **position**, it
   a. moved into a new place to live.
   b. set up its people in a special way.
   c. did not know where its people should go.
   d. let everyone go home.

9. A **rifle** is a kind of
   a. gun.
   b. car.
   c. shoe.
   d. knife.

10. A **soldier** is someone who
    a. sells clothes.
    b. works in the army.
    c. takes care of children.
    d. makes new laws.

Check your answers with the key.

Choose the best answer.

1. A **bushel** of apples is most likely to be
   a. in a pie.
   b. in a cup.
   c. on a plate.
   d. in a basket.

2. I like **October** because
   a. we can go swimming every day.
   b. we can make snowmen.
   c. the leaves on the trees are pretty colors.
   d. that is when spring begins.

3. She has a **responsible** job. That means
   a. her job is important to the people around her.
   b. she never works with her hands.
   c. her job is far from her house.
   d. she works with her husband.

4. If I am filled with **anger**, what am I most likely to do?
   a. Yell
   b. Sing
   c. Sleep
   d. Laugh

5. If I learn that my daughter is taking **drugs**, I would probably
   a. take her out to dinner.
   b. feel very upset.
   c. give her praise.
   d. study more.

6. She could **afford** that dress if she had
   a. a needle.
   b. an iron.
   c. more money.
   d. the right shoes.

7. She found out that the dress was too **expensive**. It
   a. was too long.
   b. was too big.
   c. was too colorful.
   d. cost too much money.

8. In the **future** we will take the bus. When will we take the bus?
   a. In the spring
   b. Yesterday
   c. Sometime soon
   d. Never

Check your answers with the key.

Choose the best answer.

1. When he sold the car to them on **credit**, he
   a. asked for less money.
   b. asked for more money.
   c. let them buy it and pay for it later.
   d. let them have it for free.

2. What is the boat's **crew**?
   a. Its sailors
   b. Its engines
   c. Its flags
   d. Its sails

3. I went to see some friends in my old **neighborhood**. My friends were
   a. in another country.
   b. in my house.
   c. in the part of town where I used to live.
   d. in the part of town where I live now.

4. The ocean's **tide** is made of
   a. shells.
   b. water.
   c. sand.
   d. fish.

5. If a room is **bare**, it has
   a. many windows.
   b. no door.
   c. very little in it.
   d. a fireplace.

6. You would expect **shallow** people to
   a. care a lot about other people.
   b. do what is best for someone else.
   c. do what is best for them.
   d. never tell a lie.

7. I would give my son a **stern** look if he
   a. cleaned his room.
   b. did something I told him not to do.
   c. did something nice for me.
   d. felt sick.

8. Where would you be most likely to find an **ad**?
   a. In a school book
   b. In the playground
   c. In a newspaper
   d. In the water

9. Which is an example of a **product**?
   a. The sky
   b. A sailor
   c. A boat
   d. A captain

10. You would use **toothpaste** to clean your
    a. teeth.
    b. hair.
    c. face.
    d. shoes.

Check your answers with the key.

Choose the best answer.

1. When I **adapt** to the weather, I
   a. always wear the wrong thing.
   b. always forget my umbrella.
   c. am prepared for changes in the weather.
   d. never know what the weather will be.

2. The day we had a **blizzard,**
   a. I decided to go swimming.
   b. the day was sunny and clear.
   c. there was no wind.
   d. it was very windy and snowy.

3. I could tell that the road was **icy** because
   a. there were so many hills.
   b. the road was hot.
   c. I slipped and almost fell.
   d. it was raining.

4. If you know the **temperature** of something, you know
   a. its color.
   b. how hot or cold it is.
   c. how much it weighs.
   d. how old it is.

5. An **Eskimo** child would most likely play
   a. in the snow.
   b. on the beach.
   c. on a baseball field.
   d. in the desert.

6. On a map, the northern **direction** is usually at
   a. the top.
   b. the bottom.
   c. the left.
   d. the right.

7. In the **polar** areas of the world, be careful not to
   a. get a sunburn.
   b. get lost in the desert.
   c. freeze your hands.
   d. get hit by a bus.

8. When she traveled to a new time **zone,** she was
   a. in an area where the time was different.
   b. in a machine that traveled through time.
   c. in a building with many clocks.
   d. at a party that lasted all night.

Check your answers with the key.

Choose the best answer.

1. What might make you feel **anger**?
   a. Someone gives you a present.
   b. Someone sings a song to you.
   c. Someone takes what belongs to you.
   d. Someone forgives you.

2. The **battle** was over when the
   a. lights went out.
   b. shooting stopped.
   c. door closed.
   d. school bell rang.

3. A **warrior** is good at
   a. talking.
   b. lying.
   c. singing.
   d. fighting.

4. Which of the following shows how someone might **respond** to something?
   a. A girl gets angry after her brother teases her.
   b. A man walks to work every day.
   c. A woman runs for office.
   d. A little boy wanders off and gets lost.

5. If I say that the place in which I live is a **jungle**, then I
   a. like living there.
   b. find it very cold.
   c. find it very hot.
   d. find it hard to live there.

6. What would be a hard **decision** for someone to make?
   a. Should I leave my job or stay?
   b. I want to read that book.
   c. What time does the play start?
   d. I would like to make a lot of money.

7. Someone under **stress** would probably be
   a. calm.
   b. jumpy.
   c. happy.
   d. smart.

8. If I offer you my **friendship,** I am
   a. saying that I would like to be your friend.
   b. giving you all my friends.
   c. saying that I do not want to be your friend.
   d. inviting you to meet my friends.

9. If I have a sense of **dignity,** then I feel that I am
   a. small.
   b. worthy.
   c. funny.
   d. old.

10. Which of the following would you pick for a **companion**?
    a. Someone who doesn't like you
    b. Someone you can get along with
    c. Someone who gets angry easily
    d. Someone who wants to be alone

Check your answers with the key.

Choose the best answer.

1. If you **disturb** me when I study, you will
   a. help me finish my work.
   b. be bothering me.
   c. be my friend.
   d. know just what I want.

2. She always used to **grumble** when
   a. a delicious meal was served.
   b. good friends came to visit.
   c. she did well on a test.
   d. the bus was late.

3. The bees **flutter** from flower to flower by using their
   a. eyes.
   b. honey.
   c. wings.
   d. stingers.

4. The bird began to **swoop** down upon the worm in order to
   a. eat it.
   b. sing to it.
   c. lay an egg.
   d. make a nest.

5. When I listen to the children **squawk**, it makes me feel
   a. happy.
   b. afraid.
   c. upset.
   d. like playing.

6. The people in the theater bagan to **mumble**
   a. when the actor started to sing.
   b. during the funny part.
   c. while eating popcorn.
   d. when the film broke.

7. Our bus had to take the **detour** because
   a. it ran out of gas.
   b. not enough people were on it.
   c. the road was being fixed.
   d. it was too dark to see.

8. Which of these is most important if you want to **ski**?
   a. Snow
   b. A bat
   c. A ball
   d. Rain

9. My mother filled my **thermos** with
   a. peanut butter.
   b. lunch money.
   c. milk.
   d. apples.

Check your answers with the key.

Choose the best answer.

1. Children who are playing in a **savage** way are most likely
   a. playing calmly.
   b. sharing their toys.
   c. singing loud songs.
   d. hitting and kicking each other.

2. Which of these would a **prairie** be most likely to have?
   a. Grass
   b. High mountains
   c. Forests
   d. Beaches

3. Which of these would be most likely to **ruin** a picnic?
   a. Good food
   b. Rain
   c. Tables and benches
   d. A waterfall

4. A **settler** is someone who decides to change his or her
   a. name.
   b. mind.
   c. home.
   d. job.

5. If I have a big **thirst**, I need
   a. something to eat.
   b. something to drink.
   c. to see a doctor.
   d. to lie down.

6. If I want you to be my business **partner**, I want to
   a. give my business to you.
   b. sell my business to you.
   c. share my business with you.
   d. take my business away from you.

7. I would be **rude** if I
   a. laughed at your jokes.
   b. made fun of the way you talked.
   c. told you a funny story.
   d. said we always have fun together.

8. Where would you most likely find **tears**?
   a. In your hair
   b. In your eyes
   c. In the ocean
   d. In a cup

9. I am feeling very **lonesome** today. What should I do?
   a. Go to the movies
   b. Visit a friend
   c. Read a book
   d. Go someplace where I can be alone

Check your answers with the key.

DA-1	DA-2	DA-3	DA-4	DA-5
1. a	1. c	1. d	1. c	1. b
2. a	2. d	2. a	2. a	2. c
3. d	3. a	3. b	3. b	3. a
4. c	4. b	4. b	4. d	4. c
5. c	5. b	5. d	5. b	5. a
6. a	6. b	6. c	6. a	6. c
7. a	7. a	7. a	7. d	7. d
8. d	8. c	8. b	8. c	8. a
9. a	9. b	9. d	9. b	9. b
10. c				10. a

DA-6	DA-7	DA-8	DA-9	DA-10
1. a	1. a	1. a	1. d	1. b
2. b	2. c	2. c	2. a	2. c
3. c	3. b	3. c	3. b	3. c
4. d	4. b	4. b	4. a	4. a
5. b	5. d	5. c	5. c	5. b
6. a	6. b	6. a	6. a	6. b
7. c	7. a	7. c	7. b	7. a
8. d	8. b	8. a	8. d	8. c
9. a	9. c	9. d	9. b	
		10. a	10. d	

DA-11	DA-12	DA-13	DA-14	DA-15
1. c	1. a	1. c	1. c	1. d
2. b	2. b	2. b	2. d	2. c
3. c	3. c	3. c	3. b	3. a
4. d	4. c	4. d	4. b	4. a
5. b	5. c	5. c	5. a	5. b
6. c	6. a	6. a	6. a	6. c
7. a	7. b	7. d	7. d	7. d
8. b	8. d	8. a	8. b	8. c
9. a	9. d		9. a	
	10. b		10. b	

DA-16	DA-17	DA-18	DA-19	DA-20
1. c	1. c	1. c	1. b	1. d
2. a	2. d	2. b	2. d	2. a
3. c	3. c	3. d	3. c	3. b
4. b	4. b	4. a	4. a	4. c
5. c	5. a	5. d	5. c	5. b
6. c	6. a	6. a	6. d	6. c
7. b	7. c	7. b	7. c	7. b
8. c	8. a	8. a	8. a	8. b
9. c		9. b	9. c	9. b
10. a		10. b		